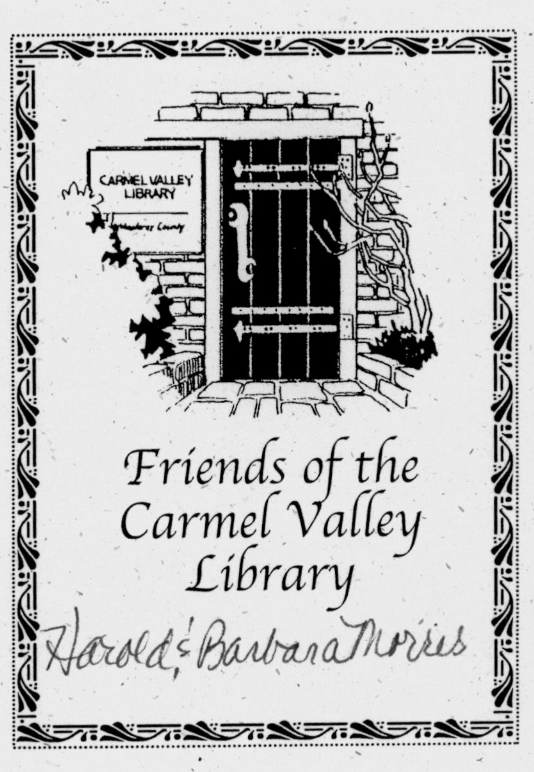
CARMEL VALLEY
LIBRARY
Friends of the
Carmel Valley
Library
Harold & Barbara Morris

Hot Type

&

Pony Wire

Hot Type
&
Pony Wire

My Life As a California Reporter from Prohibition to Pearl Harbor

John V. Young

WESTERN TANAGER PRESS
SANTA CRUZ

Text design by Michael S. Gant
Western Tanager Press
1111 Pacific Avenue
Santa Cruz, California
Printed in the United States of America

ISBN: 0–934136–05–X
Library of Congress Catalog Card: 80-81419

to
Al and Sharon Lowry
for early inspiration
& endless dedication

Contents

Illustrations

FOREWORD

This assortment of episodes and anecdotes is almost entirely a product of my memories of the country newspaper business in California in the period from 1929 to 1942, the era of the Great Depression, the end of Prohibition, the onset of World War II. Nothing was ever the same after that, in the newspaper game or anywhere else.

I have included the old *San Jose Mercury Herald* and the mercifully defunct *San Francisco News* in the category of country newspapers because at the time, in my opinion, neither had attained metropolitan size or quality. Perhaps in all fairness I should say that my attitudes and experiences all along were those of a rural reporter-cum-editor and sometimes photographer, rather than those of a big-city, grab-them-by-the-throat journalist of the Stanley Walker tradition.

In no way is this collection intended to serve as a precise historical document, although it does include some nearly forgotten lore. With the exception of some clippings and photographs I had saved from the old *Mercury Herald* and some provided recently by friends and former associates, I have relied entirely on my memory for the events depicted here. If there are errors in fact, they are errors of my memory and were made in good faith.

Some of the tales may be wrong in some detail, but none in essence, I feel certain. At one point early in the game I thought of trying to go back to read the old files of the many newspapers involved in these stories. I found to my dismay that not only had several of the newspapers disappeared entirely, but those that survived no longer preserved bound copies of back issues for more than a year or so. All the old issues were reduced to microfilm stored in libraries or elsewhere, or they were simply lost to posterity.

One or two sessions at the screen of a microfilm viewer convinced me that this way lies madness, or at least blindness. Cranking through endless pages of irrelevant material, especially in cases where I was uncertain of the year, let alone the month in question, is a chore I will happily leave to the professional historian.

I am greatly indebted to Theron Fox, Paul Conroy, Dwight Bentel and Harry Farrell of San Jose, and to Sharon and Alexander Lowry of Santa Cruz, for help and encouragement in this enterprise.

A NOTE ON TYPE

The words "hot type" in the title refer to the method of typesetting used for books, magazines and newspapers throughout most of the 20th century. Hot type machines, known as Linotype or Intertype, cast single lines of type (or "slugs") from molten metal. As a letter is struck on the keyboard, a mold for that character is released from a magazine. After all the letters for a line have been assembled, they are mechanically spaced to the proper width by thin metal wedges. The slug is then moved to the caster where molten metal is forced into the molds. After casting, the molds are returned to their magazines, ready for the next line. Since the 1950s, hot type has been increasingly supplanted by "cold type," a process by which type is reproduced photographically. Phototypesetting is generally faster than hot metal composition, but hot type work has a quality of letter shape and spacing often lacking in the newer method.

This book has been set in hot metal at Holmes Typography of San Jose on an Intertype machine. It is one of the last books to be set in this manner at Holmes. The text typeface is Times Roman.

The author as young reporter (YOUNG)

1

GETTING STARTED

THIS BOOK relates some of my personal experiences in country journalism from the stock market crash of 1929 to the early part of World War II, before network radio and TV newscasts, the automotive revolution, and computerized photo-typography altered forever the spirit and the essence of small-town newspapers.

Few if any of the events depicted here could happen again. They were products of the times: the Hoover-Roosevelt years, the end of Prohibition and the onset of the Great Depression; the Dust Bowl, the New Deal, the Lindberg kidnapping and the death of Dillinger, Social Security, the Fair Labor Standards Act and the National Labor Relations Board.

Little did I know that I was witnessing the end of an era, a hectic ending to a violent period in the nation's history that few of us who lived through it would want to see repeated; but for a young reporter much of it was fun, or so it seems in historical perspective.

Often I have been asked how I happened to become a newspaperman in the first place. "Happened" is the right word, for I did not choose the profession. I strayed or fell into it, having no notion whatever of trying to make a career of journalism until well after I found myself immersed in it up to my pockets full of pencils.

When I enrolled at San Jose State Teachers College in 1927 (it then had a student body of about 1500), I thought I wanted to become an electrical engineer. It soon became obvious, however, that about the only college-level subject with which I had any real rapport was English, written or spoken.

Since penmanship always was by far my worst subject, as far back as I can remember, I had found it necessary quite early in life to use a typewriter. In fact, my father (in despair over my illegible scrawling) gave me a typewriter when I was still in the eighth grade on the condition that I learn touch typing. I did, the hard way, out of a book, and thus became a life-long slave to the machine; but at San Jose State in 1927 typewriters for student use did not exist, and I could not afford a portable. I took a brush-up course in typing, thinking I might thereby bootleg the use of a classroom machine in off-hours, but that scheme did not work. The course did, however, help my typing speed.

Finally I found an ancient Underwood in the office of the college weekly publication, which only in charity could be called a newspaper. In return for the use of the machine when it was not in demand, I agreed to type up the handwritten copy turned in by the student staff. Their typing was even worse than their handwriting (or mine) and the printers would not touch the copy if it was not at least legible. In order to make the copy not only legible but intelligible, I found I had to rewrite most of it: sift out the bad grammer, correct the spelling, add punctuation—in short, edit it. (I knew nothing about journalism, but I did know English composition. My mother was hipped on the subject and saw to it that my brother and I were acquainted with gerunds long before we knew about sex. To this day I cannot split an infinitive without glancing nervously over my shoulder.)

I should not have been so surprised as I was when I found myself in the job of managing editor, which meant I had to write just about all the news and editorials, scrounge photos, read proof, write heads, make up the pages, and put the paper to bed at the downtown print shop. The printers were so glad to see a student editor who knew an apostrophe from a catastrophe that they became most obliging in teaching me what I had to know about their end of the business. I even learned to read type upside down, a necessary skill for any makeup editor in the days of hot type.

It was as a student editor that I suffered my first exposure to the perils of fearless journalism in a closed society, long before the days of militant student protests.

The college had hired a new president, a distinguished-looking gentleman whose given name was Thomas D. In his inaugural address to the student body, he urged everybody to "call me Tom," an unheard-of innovation in liberality for a time when college presidents ranked right up there with bankers and judges on the social scale. So, in our next issue of the paper, we referred to the president as "Dr. Thomas D. (Call Me Tom) MacQuarrie." He did not like it, and so informed me in positive terms.

Some time later a rumor went around the campus that the football coach was about to be fired. The president's office issued a bland statement to the effect that the coach was resigning because of ill health. But the coach, when confronted with this statement, said he never had felt better in his life.

In the interests of truth and fair play, we ran both statements side by side on the front page of the next issue. They made interesting reading. Again, the president was unhappy, not to mention downright hostile. He gave me a simple choice: abandon my scurrilous attacks on the Establishment or be kicked out of college. In 1929, he no doubt could have made it stick.

I chose a third route, a slight compromise. I gave up the editorship, not having any real commitment to a journalistic career in the first place. I think I knew my days in that place were numbered anyhow.

(Come to think of it, I had had a still earlier encounter with the power of Authority over Freedom of the Press. In either my junior or senior year at Los Gatos high school, I was editor of a putative school newspaper, a one-page mimeographed effort that was tolerated—briefly—by the administration.

(It died suddenly after one issue carried a perfectly innocent front-page piece no more than an inch long. It reported on the arrival of a new child in the family of the vice-principal, a man named Dailey. I think it was his sixth or seventh blessed event. Our report on the happy occasion was headed simply: A DAILEY EVENT. I thought it was pretty cute, but Mr. Dailey did not. Little did he realize how close he came to blighting the career of a budding, if unconscious, journalist.)

When I left college after two years, partly from lack of money and partly from lack of direction, I still was not thinking at all of becoming a newspaperman. The one journalism course I had taken in college was a disaster, taught by an elderly pedant who, I imagine, had never so much as smelled printer's ink.

I had learned that I certainly was never going to become an engineer, but I had only a fuzzy idea of what I did want to do with my life. My best guess at the time was that I might like to become an advertising copywriter, a glamorous and reputedly well-paid vocation in that glittering era just before the Crash.

Through an uncle who had some connections, I wrangled interviews with two or three of San Francisco's leading advertising agencies. From each I learned what should have been obvious: I needed some practical experience, first-hand, in the desires and habits of the general public. This, I was told, could best be obtained by door-to-door selling or by working on a small-town newspaper as an advertising salesman and copywriter.

Door-to-door selling I could not see at all, but I knew even less about how to go about getting a job on a newspaper of any size or shape. Finally, the editor of *Sunset*, I think it was, took pity on me and directed me to the office of the California Newspaper Publisher's Association, a trade organization that served small-town newspapers and ran a free employment agency.

The first job I was given a shot at was a combination one—editor and advertising manager and circulation manager (in fact, the entire staff other than a lone printer) of the *Pleasanton Times,* a nearly defunct weekly in a tiny foothill town in Alameda County. I lasted there about six weeks, failing (as I now recall) not so much from any lack of journalistic ability as from a total inability to sell advertising. In self defense, I might mention that the stock market had just crashed in the fall of 1929 and small-town merchants were all hiding their cash in coffee cans.

After a couple more false starts in the business end, I grabbed at a chance to be interviewed for a job as a reporter on a small daily paper in an industrial town named Pittsburg, fifty miles up-country from San Francisco. I had never been in Pittsburg and knew nothing about the place, but at that moment in history I would not have cared if it had been Timbuktu.

I was getting pretty desperate, wondering (as I knew my family and friends were) whether I could ever keep a job, since I had gone through three in four months. Also, it was beginning to dawn on me, dimly, that if I had any talent or experience of value to anyone, it would have to be as a reporter, or reporter-cum-editor, and certainly not as a salesman.

That discovery should not have taken so long. The only scholastic honor I ever won was in a college essay contest. My entry was a piece of straight, factual reporting on my experiences working in a fruit cannery during the summer. Then there was my brief but useful experience as editor of the college weekly, which at least in the editorial process did not suffer all that much from any small-town newspaper, or so I thought.

I arrived in Pittsburg, California, one midnight in early January, 1930. The train deposited me in pouring rain at a closed depot a mile from town. Of course, there was no taxi, even if I could have afforded one. Wet to the skin, I lugged my heavy suitcase and weary carcass to the front door of the old Los Medanos Hotel, where I was finally able to arouse the night clerk by nearly kicking the door down.

I do not remember much about the room except that it was warm, and I was able to dry out before I fell into bed. It was just as well that I was bone-weary, for the fatigue enabled me to sleep despite the fact that I was scared silly. I knew that if I blew this one, my chances of getting another referral from the California Newspaper Publishers Association were nil, and that with the Depression in full swing, jobs of any kind were vanishing.

When I reported for work the next morning in the dingy little newspaper office on a side street in unbeautiful downtown Pittsburg, I was not only scared, but appalled to find three other candidates for the job. In my youth and innocence, I had assumed that I was to be the one and only.

The boss—a former Hearst newspaperman and retired Army officer named John Tiedeman, an imposing figure with a ramrod spine and a fierce mustache—sent each of us out on a news assignment. (It was one way to fill the paper, I thought.) My task was to go to city hall and see the chief of police about an important arrest.

I forget the details, but I do remember that the kindly old chief, who had been head of both the police and the fire departments for thirty years, realized my predicament and all but dictated the story. He had had a lot more experience than I had. I scribbled some notes, thanked him profusely, and hurried back to the office to bang out my story while it was still fresh.

Then I was told to write a head on it, and did so. That was the easy part. The hard part was waiting to see what was going to happen next. After an eternity or two, John Tiedeman called me into his office to tell me I had the job, and could start at once at twenty dollars a week. In fact, I had already started.

I was dumfounded, in view of the competition from men obviously older and more experienced than I, a very green twenty year old who had never worked on a daily newspaper before, or anywhere else long enough to count. What I was about to find out was that I had been chosen solely on the basis of my typing speed, then about fifty words a minute. The important fact was that I used all ten fingers, while the other three candidates were hunt-and-peck artists. That kind of typing was good enough for most situations, but not, as it turned out, for what lay in store for me.

Thus began the episode of the pony wire, and thirteen years of small-town journalism.

2

THE PONY WIRE

SHORTLY BEFORE noon the morning I was hired by the *Pittsburg Dispatch,* after doing some routine rewrite chores, I was introduced to an infernal device called the pony wire. I had noticed an extra typewriter at a corner desk with a pair of headphones hung over it, but had not given it any thought.

Some background is needed here. Before small-town daily newspapers had teletype machines, they obtained their wire service (press association) news of the world by telephone. The equipment consisted of a stripped-down typewriter with only three rows of keys (all capital letters), a pair of padded headphones, a talk-back microphone controlled by a foot switch (to cut out typewriter noise), and a presumably fast typist at the keyboard.

Promptly at noon every working day, the phone rang and a voice that said it was United Press in San Francisco called the roll of the newspapers hooked into that particular tank-town circuit. There were nine on our circuit, eight of them old hands. I was the ninth.

With no further ado, United Press began to recite the day's

ration of hot news, at a speed I was to find out was 100 words a minute for 30 minutes! Instant panic paralyzed my brain and my fingers. If I live to be 110, I'll never forget that awful moment.

The keys all piled up in a bird's nest. Frantically trying to untangle the mess, I yelled "Stop" into the microphone. It was dead. Then I remembered the foot switch and stomped on it, yelling "Stop" again. Instantly my ears were blasted by eight voices in unison, telling me to get the hell off the line. United Press said "Sorry" and went right on reading at 100 words a minute.

As I soon learned, the problem was that all the national and international news any of us were going to get, and we needed all we could get to fill gaping pages and headlines, had to be acquired in those precious thirty minutes. Overtime was too expensive to consider, nor was there time for it. Press time was only an hour and a half away and the printers, who had the patience of hungry barracudas, were screaming for copy.

So I stopped yelling and did the best I could, which was terrible, a mishmash of abbreviated typing interspersed with handwritten notes. The boss was looking on, chewing his nails. Happily, I was aware that if anyone else in the place could have taken the pony wire, I would not be doing it. Bad as I was, I was just about indispensable in that situation, at least for the moment.

Of course, the paper was late getting out that day, and the next. It might not have come out at all that first day, I suspect, had it not been for a bit of spontaneous altruism on the part of one of the other pony wire participants, or perhaps I should say acrobats. He called up in the middle of my muddle to offer to fill me in anything I might have missed, as he put it. What I had missed was just about everything. He dictated (slowly) enough for me to get by.

Then he told me how to beat the game. He pointed out that most of the so-called hot news on the pony wire was actually no more than a rehash of the stories appearing in the morning San Francisco newspapers, which arrived in Pittsburg shortly before noon. He suggested that I could get by, until I got up to full speed (if I ever did), by taking down only the first paragraph or two and clipping the rest from the morning papers. The boss, who was something of a journalistic purist, did not like the idea very well, but it was better than no copy at all and it kept me alive long enough to do the job.

For all that, I have no idea how I survived those first few days and weeks. I must have, somehow, for I held that job for more than a year. In sheer desperation I pushed my typing speed up to the requisite 100 words a minute and a little beyond. That was not a net speed without errors, of course—the linotypists did not care so long as the copy was reasonably legible. They taught me so tricks, too, like abbreviating international to IXL, unconstitutional to UXL, and the obvious shortening of Los Angeles to LA, New York to NY, etc.

Nonetheless, what now follows may be hard to believe for anyone who has not been a telegrapher or had a pony wire initiation, although I suppose in essence the facility is not much different from that which any instrumental musician learns as a matter of course—how to disassociate one hand from the other and both from the conscious mind. Not being a musician, I suspect the pony wire is easier.

At the end of a couple of months I was not only able to keep up with the pony wire without a break and without depending on the morning newspapers, but had time to eat my lunch while it was going on, even answering the telephone if nobody else was around. I found I could store up two or three paragraphs in my head while I did something else, then put on a burst of speed to catch up, typing like mad on one bunch of words while listening to another bunch coming in over the wire.

The process became entirely mechanical, as it had to be. If I stopped to realize what I was doing, panic set in, but not for long. Once I took down a story, edited it, wrote a head on it, and later read proof on it, but was not aware until the paper came out that it was about a distant relative of mine who had blown his head off with a shotgun. The name was perfectly familiar, but it simply had not registered in the process.

Toward the end of my stay on the Pittsburg paper, I trained a high school girl who was a typing champion to take the wire, which gave me the chance to leave the office and cover a courthouse story at the county seat in Martinez. While I was there I dropped in to visit the editor of the local daily paper, one of the eight other men whom I had known only as disembodied voices answering the roll call at noon every working day. I was particularly interested in this man, for I had identified him with some singularly machinelike typing I had heard when he accidentally left his microphone switch open. (By then, each of us on the pony wire circuit could identify most of the others by the sound of their typing, which was as distinctive as a telegrapher's "fist.")

When I walked in, he was finishing up on the pony wire, typing mostly with one hand while he munched on a sandwich and turned the pages of the *Saturday Evening Post* with the other. He waved me to a seat while he finished typing, which took several minutes after he had taken off the headphones.

I never saw anything like that typing, before or since. Clean copy, without an error, flowed across the paper as if the words were being squirted out of a nozzle, a steady rhythm broken only by the rapid-fire slamming of the return carriage.

When he stopped, I asked him how fast he had been going. He said it probably was up around 144 words a minute when he was using both hands.

"But isn't that world champion speed?" I asked.

He shrugged and opened a desk drawer to show me a case full of medals. "I was the world champion," he said, "but there wasn't any money in it."

After that I thought that had I been witness to such a performance during my first days on the pony wire, I would have bolted from the place like a scalded cat and gone back to picking prunes.

Incidentally, that speed demon on the typewriter was the one who helped me out that first day on the wire—being the only one on the circuit who had time to be helpful in the middle of the day.

Later in my newspaper career I had many opportunities to watch a truly virtuoso performance on the keyboard in the telegraph room at the *San Jose Mercury Herald*—a performance that put to shame my pony wire acrobatics.

In the early 1930s that submetropolitan newspaper had long since outgrown the pony wire, but it still had, in addition to a row of teletype machines, what was known as an open sports wire. This was an old-fashioned dot-and-dash telegraph system over which last-minute news was transmitted in Morse code directly from the scene of action, such as the ringside at a major prize fight.

At the receiving end, of course, there had to be an old-fashioned telegrapher to translate the clickety-clacks into typewritten words, and there was, in the person of dapper Eddie McManiman. Eddie was a man of great dignity and sartorial elegance—and indeterminate age, my guess was that he was in his late sixties or early seventies when I first knew him. He was a master craftsman, one of the last of his line.

Eddie liked to smoke but smoking was prohibited in the austere premises of the newspaper in those days, along with drinking and taking the Lord's name in vain. So when the craving became too strong, Eddie would leave his office on the second floor and stroll downstairs to an alley directly under his window, there to meet other nicotine addicts. He always put an empty tobacco can behind the telegraph sounder to amplify the clicks and left a window open. For all his mature years, Eddie had sharp ears, finely tuned to the sound of the key by his long years of experience.

When the code letters for the newspaper (SJ: ••• —•—•) clattered in on the sounder, Eddie would take a last puff on his cigarette, extinguish the stub under his foot, and sedately march back up the two flights of stairs to his office. I never was able to hear the telegraph key clicking on those stairs, but Eddie could.

Meanwhile the sender, knowing Eddie of old, had not waited

for an acknowledgement but had started to send the story. If it was about a prize fight, it might well have proceeded to round two or even round three before Eddie reached his typewriter.

Once there he still did not hurry, but first hung up his jacket, donned a pair of cardboard cuffs to protect his immaculate, starched shirt, adjusted his bow tie, inserted a piece of copy paper in the machine, and then started typing. He always sat bolt upright, always with aplomb. He did not seem to type very fast but always it was fast enough to catch up with the wire after a little while. Sometimes the fight would end while Eddie was still typing the blow-by-blow account of a couple of rounds earlier.

If anyone poked his head in the door to ask about the fight, Eddie would give a concise oral report on its current status, without interrupting the even flow of his finger work. He never seemed to miss a beat, or he was very good at improvising.

For a long report, such as a World Series baseball game, Eddie would settle in for an extended session by eating his lunch and reading the *Saturday Evening Post* (yes, just like my friend on the pony wire at Martinez). Incidentally, Eddie supplemented his salary by serving as a magazine subscription agent, along with some other interesting little sidelines. Typically, his typing often ran one or more plays behind the action.

Eddie was gone, along with the open sports wire, when I returned to the *Mercury Herald* in 1937, and I never did learn what had become of him. Presumably he retired. Eddie and his ancient craft were victims of the wave of mechanical innovation that started with the linotype and probably will not end until reporters and editors are replaced by robots, and brain waves bounced off satellites supersede the printed page.

3

AUNT BELLA BAKER

MUCH OF WHAT HAPPENED during my thirteen hectic months on the *Pittsburg Dispatch* has always been a blur in my memory. Usually there was no scarcity of news in a town of 10,000 full of unemployed steel workers and fishermen. Violence was commonplace—murders, mayhem, a train robbery, fatal accidents, fires, explosions, a bank president defaulting with the funds in a neighboring town. It was also Prohibition time, and bootleggers and hijackers were in their element in that riverside city off the main routes, with a maze of sloughs and islands for hiding places.

One of my problems was that the news came in unpredictable bunches, not in any regular flow, never when I most needed it. Even so, my boss, who had been a Hearst make-up editor and never got over it, used to give me a front-page dummy the first thing each morning, with banner headlines, column headings, and pictures neatly sketched in, all with total disregard of what the day's offering of news might be. It was simply up to me to find something to fit the dummy, somewhere, somehow, like trying to find a body to fit a ready-made suit of an odd size, six days a week.

Sometimes the banner headlines so indicated would have been

suitable for a mass murder (in a type size usually referred to as Second Coming) when the hottest item on the incoming wire might be a two-day-old train wreck in Pocatello, Idaho.

On the other hand, the layouts the boss provided used up so much space on the front page, I did not have to find all that much actual front-page copy and could use more of what I had to fill the gaping inside pages. They went to press early and often were more of a problem than the front page.

A make-up problem on one inside page every Saturday resulted directly in an episode that still stands out clearly in my memory. I think of it (with a shudder) as "The Life and Death of Aunt Bella Baker." I did not know it at the time, of course, but she (or it) could be considered an early forerunner of Ann Landers. Just so narrowly did I miss fame and fortune—perhaps.

It came about like this: Our paper was printed in eight-column format, but for some reason, probably economic, our Saturday comics came in seven-column mats. This left a column to be filled up early each Saturday, with something appropriate to a funny page if possible.

A few times when we were short of copy for that column and could find nothing to steal from out-of-town newspapers, we used a sports story or some society notes, but that went over with a dull thud with the parties concerned, all of whom much preferred front-page exposure. Besides, we needed something with no time angle.

I never had time to go out and dig up amusing features, and the ones that came in from volunteers often were not printable. Since Pittsburg was in no way in a farming area, we had no offerings of three-legged chickens or two-headed calves.

Then I had an earthshaking idea. Why not a tongue-in-cheek column of advice to the lovelorn? It was not an entirely original idea, since something of the sort appeared now and then in one of the San Francisco newspapers, in a humorous column called Cook's Cuckoos (or was it Kook's Kookoos?). Mr. Cook's ficticious lovelorn editor was dubbed Aunt Bella Baker.

We adopted Aunt Bella without an apology to Mr. Cook,

figuring that about the last newspaper he would ever see was ours. We selected a wire-service photo of a sultry-looking Italian movie actress of mature years, had a thumbnail cut made of her mug, and with appropriate fanfare launched her alleged column in that blank space on the Saturday comic page.

At first, I wrote both the letters and the answers, managing in my initial enthusiasm (and youthful innocence) to work up a fair-sized backlog of what I hoped were suitably subtle and also funny contributions. About the third week after the first column appeared, however, we started getting letters in the mail, first a trickle and then a veritable flood. Sometimes we got two or three in a day, a landslide for a paper whose daily mail consisted mainly of subscription cancellations.

They certainly looked like serious letters. Some seemed deadly serious, like: "Dear Aunt Bella—I think I am going to have a baby and I am not married or anything. I am sixteen. Please tell me what to do." At first, I thought our dear readers were merely going along with the gag, and I started to write appropriate replies. At this point, however, I had second thoughts (having been burned a few times on other stunts). I took the letters to my boss, John Tiedeman, who had been burned about every way there is to get burned in the newspaper business during his long career.

What if, I asked, some of the letters were for real?

He reacted as if somebody had stuck him with a cattle prod. The answer, he agreed instantly, was that we had to assume that *all* the letters were serious even if we did have our leg pulled now and then in the process.

Tiedeman and his wife, who was also a newspaper veteran, took over the chore of writing answers to all the letters that seemed worth answering. They were quickly out of my reach, those pitiful pleas, since I was still only a very green twenty-one and quite damp behind the ears. Besides, I was much too busy, now that the stunt had turned into something like the Sorcerer's Apprentice and his proliferating brooms. I never would have suspected that a small town could harbor so many desperate souls, or that so many of our subscribers ever read anything except the headlines and the sports page.

Nobody seemed to mind that the letters and answers appeared on the funny page (or the page was not all that funny), although the position made no sense. We even thought of moving it up front somewhere, since it was so popular. Then the publisher and his wife wanted to go to Hawaii to a newspaper convention, and we had to come to a great decision. The answer was to do in Aunt Bella. We made it look like an accident, by solemnly reporting on the front page, under a Los Angeles dateline, that the old girl had gone to her reward under a truck while on vacation in Hollywood. As there was simply nobody (but nobody) to take her place, we had reluctantly decided to discontinue the column and return all letters, the story said.

Once more we underrated the need people have for free advice. There could not have been a louder outcry if we had stopped running the horoscope, or the crossword puzzle, or some other priceless item. Letters continued to come in for months, including several from local matrons who felt qualified to take Aunt Bella's place by virtue of having survived several spouses each. Probably the best qualified was one of the local madams, but we were afraid she was too well known in her own right.

In time, the tumult and the shouting died away, but not before I was embarrassed on several occasions by being called Aunt Bella to my face by comparative strangers on the street. There are no secrets in small towns.

4

THE POLICE CHIEF'S UNTIMELY END

IT SEEMS TO ME that small-town newspapers are more prone to fall victim to Murphy's Law than most other small businesses. Murphy's Law says that in any given set of circumstances, the worst possible combination inevitably will ensue. In other words, things always get fouled up. Perhaps this is because in general small-town newspapers are understaffed, disorganized, and never have time enough to do anything just right. Furthermore, the results are painfully apparent to the local public.

My best (or worst) example of this phenomenon comes all too vividly to mind even now. It is the story of how Murphy's Law engineered the untimely demise of the chief of police of Pittsburg, at least in the columns of our newspaper. He did not really die, but we almost did.

This sort of thing could only have happened to a small daily paper in the era of hot type, when all the copy was set on Linotype machines, which produced metal slugs (lines of type) which in turn were assembled in metal forms to be placed on the press. In these days of computerized typesetting, it might be difficult to find a Linotype machine outside a museum, let alone one actually in use in the production of a newspaper, so you'll just have to take my word for this peculiar and now archaic process, the parent of both ETAOIN and SHRDLU. (etaoin shrdlu: a combination of letters set by running a finger down the first and then the second left-hand vertical bank of six keys of a Linotype machine to produce a temporary slug not intended to appear in the final printing.)

To get back to the machinations of Murphy, when the composing room ran short of metal for type on occasions like special editions, the printers dashed around frantically looking in odd corners for forgotten galleys of type that could be melted down to feed the hungry machines. Or if nobody was looking, the type might be shoved into a gaping column as is. A chance like that Murphy could not miss.

Now, to backtrack a bit more, remember the kindly old chief of police of Pittsburg, the one who helped me out on that first day on the job? Well, he had a heart attack and appeared to be at death's door. While the mourners arrived from near and far, we put together a whole front-page obituary, ready to roll, with his picture and life history and comments from leading citizens—everything except the date and hour of his actual departure from this mortal coil. But the chief had survived more serious troubles than a mere heart attack. A friend smuggled a jug of red wine into his room, and he got better. In fact, he went back to work. We had to tear up the page because we needed the metal and the table space, but we kept the galley of type giving his life history, just in case. It gathered dust on a back shelf for months.

Then one day came a special edition, extra pages to fill, extra type required, extra printers from out of town to help out. One page was short about a column of type. One of the extra printers found what he needed on a back shelf and popped it into place. You have already guessed what it was. Under a standing head used for an occasional sports feature, there it was:

SPEAKING OF SPORT
by Allen Getty

> Chief of Police Scudero was 56 years old at the time of his death. Born in Italy, he came to this country . . .

And so on for about 700 words. There was no way to get the papers back once they hit the street, but I did manage to beat the delivery boy to the city hall with a copy to show to the chief before anyone else did.

You know, he almost had another heart attack laughing over the boo-boo. He made me promise to save him fifty copies of the paper to send to his relatives and friends who might not see it otherwise. He said it was the funniest thing that had ever happened to him.

Back at the office, however, it was not so funny. The phone calls started within half an hour and continued all night and well into the following week. It was like an endless nightmare. The chief, it seemed, was related to virtually everyone of Italian descent in the county, and their numbers were legion. Those that did not see the paper soon heard from those that did. A legion of friends joined the attack on the paper as well, either on the phone or in person.

In vain we tried to explain that it was an accident, not a joke, but the explanations fell on deaf ears among people who had not the foggiest idea of how a newspaper was put together. For that matter, they could not understand why we had an obituary in type in the first place, since most of them did not know the chief had even been ill. After all, he was obviously hale and hearty.

I really believe that had not the chief himself interceded on our behalf with some of the more vociferous of his admirers, the reaction might have reached the stage of physical violence.

Weeks passed before the excitement finally died and we stopped losing subscribers. The episode was picked up by "Cook's Cuckoos" column in the *San Francisco Chronicle* (the one from which we had stolen Aunt Bella Baker earlier), and for a time I achieved minor fame in San Francisco Bay area newspaper circles as the editor who killed the chief of police.

Long ago I stopped trying to explain exactly what happened that day, and now, even after nearly half a century, it still does not seem to me to have been all that funny. I might add that never again did I keep an obituary in type on any newspaper where I had control of such items.

5

THE NAME OF THE GAME

IN ORDER TO AUGMENT our miniscule salaries, newspapermen like myself in small towns like Pittsburg in the 1930s commonly took on moonlight jobs as part-time correspondents (called stringers) for metropolitan and county seat newspapers and for the wire services. At one time I worked simultaneously for several—the *Oakland Tribune, San Francisco Call-Bulletin, Stockton Record,* United Press.

When news was scarce, we would sometimes accentuate it, working in tandem with other newsmen, taking turns making and breaking headline copy strictly for the early editions of out-of-town newspapers. Much of the stuff never saw the light of day locally.

(Those were the days when big city newspapers still depended more on street sales than on home delivery for their major circulation. They issued numerous editions, sometimes less than an hour apart, with huge headlines to catch the eye of the men going to work or coming home. Often the headlined story in the first edition would disappear inside or out of the paper by the second edition. Some of the so-called editions were no more than revisions of the front page alone, called replates. This was sometimes called "grab 'em by the throat" journalism. It gradually disappeared after radio took the cream off the news, even before TV.)

I recall one story that was more or less typical of the time. I had a prebreakfast call from a friendly deputy sheriff about a car found just out of town all smashed up, with blood on the dashboard, booze in a broken jug, but no body. A reporter from the rival local paper and I borrowed a car and hurried to the scene, where we found a smashed-up black sedan of the kind favored by gangsters, blood and teeth on the dashboard, and the broken bottle. The car had out-of-town plates.

We tossed a coin and I won. For the first edition of the *San Francisco Call-Bulletin* I phoned in a possible hijacking-murder-kidnapping, quoting the deputy sheriff. He did not mind at all. In fact, he would have posed for a picture if we had had a camera.

In the next edition of the competing *San Francisco News* my opposite number refuted the story, quoting a local dentist to the effect that he had treated a traveling salesman for smashed teeth incurred when he went to sleep at the wheel while drunk and ran off the road. We had both suspected this to be the case, but had carefully refrained from checking local dentists until that first edition was safely on the street.

Since the guy was from out of town with no local connections, we did not bother to write a line for our own papers. The *Call-Bulletin* did not care about the story's blowing up. It had sold papers on the streets of San Francisco, and that was the name of the game in the hey-day of Hearst journalism.

Not all my sideline reporting for other newspapers was that hectic, or that flimsy of substance. I still have a warm feeling for the *Stockton Record,* which occasionally accepted a solid story from Pittsburg or one of the other small towns on the fringe of its circulation area in Contra Costa County, and paid quite well for it.

One morning a local businessman with whom I had become friendly called to tell me he had just come through Brentwood, a small town farther upriver, and had noticed some excitement. There was a crowd in front of the bank, he said, and a notice was being posted on the door. There were several sheriff's cars around, also. Since this was during the Depression and banks were starting to fail, it sounded like a big story—but one well out of my reach. I telephoned the *Stockton Record* to pass on the tip, along with a couple of suggestions from my friend about whom to call for information.

It turned out to be quite a story, at that. The bank president had absconded with some of the funds, then had suffered an attack of conscience and tried to commit suicide by driving his car off a loading dock at the railroad depot. All he had succeeded in doing was to wreck the car and break his nose. He fled on foot, leaving a trail of blood.

I forget the rest of the gory details, but the story needed no embellishment. It went on for several days, with many repercussions in the community. The *Stockton Record* paid me space rates (by the column inch) for every bit of that story, since my tip had given the paper a clean scoop. The little we carried in our own paper on the story we took from the pony wire—Brentwood was not in our circulation area and we had some sort of local doings that took precedence on the front page at the time.

Another fairly lucrative story for the *Stockton Record* literally fell into my lap without warning one day just at our press time. There was a slight shudder in the building, and the whole front window of the office fell in. Fortunately, the venetian blinds were down so that nobody was hurt by the glass, most of which landed on or around my desk.

Along with everyone else, I ran out into the street, thinking a big earthquake was in progress. But the blast turned out to be from a refinery forty miles away, where a large fuel tank had exploded, shattering windows for miles around on a hit-or-miss basis. My telephone tip to the *Stockton Record* beat the wire service report by more than an hour and was in time to catch that paper's final edition. The *Record* again paid me for all the coverage that followed, the only paper I ever worked for that was so scrupulous about paying stringers.

On the strength of these and a few other windfalls, I had an idea of quitting my job on the *Pittsburg Dispatch* and setting myself up as a full-time free-lance stringer for as many newspapers and wire services as I could line up. (The phrase "conflict of interest" had not penetrated the hinterlands in those days.)

But before I could take the plunge, other events took the decision out of my hands, as the finale of the following episode will disclose.

6

THE ROSE BOWL

NOT QUITE EVERYTHING I put my hand to in those hectic days resulted in disaster, or was the result of one. Now and then Murphy took a day off, or was busy elsewhere messing up the life of another country editor.

As I mentioned earlier, Pittsburg, California, in 1930 was a wild-eyed sports town if nothing else. I believe we could have filled almost the entire paper with sports news, had the material been available, without losing a subscriber.

Excitement always ran high in town over such major sports events as the annual Rose Bowl game at Pasadena. Before the days of television and FM radio, however, eager fans had to sit on Saturday afternoons with their ears glued to a noisy AM radio, trying to sift the news from the static, or they had to wait for the Sunday San Francisco papers to arrive about noon the next day. There was no local radio station at the time, and reception from the Bay Area was a sometimes thing.

Probably the best long-distance radio reception in town was

available at the Montgomery Ward store across the street from our office, by virtue of a high antenna on top of a four-story building (a skyscraper for Pittsburg) and some rather expensive multi-tube radio sets in the showroom. That proximity to our newspaper gave rise to an idea of mine, one which the Montgomery Ward store manager accepted with enthusiasm. The newspaper management also accepted, only because, I suspect, Montgomery Ward was a major advertiser.

According to my plan, we put the Saturday afternoon paper to bed early on the day of the Rose Bowl game, then immediately laid out two new front pages. One held an eight-column banner in huge type which said: STANFORD WINS (with space for the score). The other said DARTMOUTH WINS (or perhaps it was Michigan that year—the difference is immaterial now). We hoped the game would not end in a tie, and it didn't.

Across the street at Ward's, in a corner of a top-floor room which had been partitioned off for the occasion, I sat at a desk with two typewriters and a pair of headphones (borrowed from the pony wire) connected to Ward's biggest and best radio set, something called, I think, an Airline de luxe Super Heterodyne. The store manager and some of his cronies were listening in the main room. The headphones shut out the noise of their revelry.

On one typewriter I had planned to take down the entire game, play by play, a journalistic tour-de-force usually afforded only by metropolitan papers with direct wire connections to the scene of the action. On the other machine I had proposed to write the highlights as they occurred and a running general narrative. I had virtually memorized the names of the players on both teams and had their rosters in front of me with such vital statistics as height, weight, chest measurement and scoring record of each of the contestants (but not which deodorant they preferred).

Beforehand, I had experimented with following a football game play-by-play on a typewriter, and had found it absurdly easy.

Out of all the rapid-fire chatter the sports announcers were (and still are today) obliged to employ to fill in the time, very little had to be transcribed in order to tell the story.

It would go something like this: "Jones has the ball—it looks like a quarter-back sneak off right tackle—no—it's a fake—he's off and running—no—look OUT! It's a loose ball!—there's a big pileup. . . . Jones still has the ball. I think they are bringing out the marker. No—the referee is waving them back. Jones seems to have lost a yard. . . ."

So went the radio, at times just short of hysteria. But all I had to type out, while the players were getting unscrambled, was about a dozen words saying that Jones lost a yard in a quarterback sneak off tackle. On the other typewriter I might write that Stanford lost a good chance to get into field goal range when Jones ran into his own right tackle, or that the Dartmouth fullback tackled the referee and threw him for a loss.

Even without my pony wire experience, the job would have been a breeze. As it was, I found the process almost boring what with time-outs, huddles, penalties, injuries, intermissions and commercial breaks. As fast as I pounded out the copy in short "takes" (about half of a typing page each), a copyboy ran them across the way to be set in type and brought back proofs, which I had plenty of time to read. An extra set of proofs gave me a quick reference to what had gone before.

Within a few minutes after the game ended, the last of the copy was in type. All we had to do was to fill in the numbers in the big headlines (after making sure we had the right one), add a final paragraph to the running story to cover the final seconds, and go to press. I think we were on the street within forty-five minutes of the final gun, and the ink was scarcely dry before the newsboys were shouting "Wuxtra" on the street. We sold out the entire press run in a couple of hours.

A few of the local skeptics admitted to me later that they had waited to compare our account with those in the San Francisco papers the next day before paying off their bets, on the chance that we had faked the whole thing, a fine testimonial to our credibility rating. But nobody ever questioned how we managed to get into print so fast with an enormous photo of the final plunge over the goal line that wrapped up the game for whoever won. Mind you, we were nearly 400 miles from Pasadena, wire photo service was still in the offing, and besides, the nearest photoengraving plant was forty miles away and closed on Saturday afternoons.

Nevertheless, our four-column photo, taking up about a quarter of the front page, was there to behold. Actually, it was a photo of some other player in some other game at some other time, selected from our photo-mat feature service. (Our photos came in the form of mats, which were then cast in metal and mounted on wood blocks for use on a flatbed press.) A light tap with a hammer took care of the number on his jersey, and our rather muddy printing process sufficiently obscured the rest of the detail, including all the faces that were visible. As you may be aware, when you have seen one football pileup you have seen them all, especially when they are printed on a worn-out flatbed press on newsprint paper from a mat reproduction of a 60-line-screen engraving.

Come to think of it, I do not believe we actually went so far as to state in the caption just who was doing what to whom—we left all that to the reader's imagination. The caption said something like "CRUCIAL ACTION IN THE BIG GAME." Fortunately, the final play, or the winning one, was neither a forward pass nor a field goal—but it would have been easy enough to write a new caption had it been needed.

To this day, when I listen to the radio or watch a TV sports announcer make his obligatory disclaimer to the fact that reproduction or rebroadcast of the program for commercial purposes without prior permission of the network is strictly prohibited, etc., etc., I think of that sneaky extra edition in that forlorn little industrial city. In particular I think of how smoothly it all went and how proud I was of the result, entirely without a pang of conscience over the piracy of the coverage and the chicanery in the matter of the photo. It all seemed like just good clean fun at the time, with perhaps a tiny profit for the paper.

My reward for all the extra effort, other than personal pride of accomplishment, was typical of the time and place. Not only did I not receive any bonus or any other recognition at all, but when a short time later I contracted pneumonia and asked for time off to go to the hospital, I was fired out of hand. I should mention that the publisher then was no longer John Tiedeman, who had sold out and left, but a new man who had little interest in sports, and not very much use for me.

He explained that a man had to be tough to get along in the newspaper game, and if I couldn't cut the mustard physically, I should seek an easier kind of work, like selling notions in a dry goods store. He did have a point—I was in no shape to fight pneumonia after thirteen months of long hours, short sleep, far too many cigarettes, greasy-spoon lunch-counter food and bootleg booze.

I went home for a long siege of illness. In the days before antibiotics, pneumonia was often a killer even for people in top physical condition, which I was not.

7

HOLY CITY'S LAST HURRAH

My next job after Pittsburg still seems, in retrospect, like a miracle, a prime example of the advantage of being in the right place at the right time. In some ways, it was about the best newspaper job I ever had and certainly the most pleasant.

I was at home on my parents' fruit-and-chicken ranch south of San Jose, between Campbell and Los Gatos, in the early spring of 1931. I was twenty-two, broke, and recuperating slowly from that long bout of pneumonia that had chased me out of Pittsburg. The Santa Clara Valley was a beautiful place to be at that time of year, in those halcyon days before high-rise apartment buildings and sprawling shopping centers had supplanted the vast acreages of fruit blossoms spreading their fragrant canopies over fields of mustard and California poppies.

The large insect in the ointment for me was the fact that not only did I have no job, I was also not in very good shape to go looking for one even if I had known where to look. The Depression was in full swing; newspapers were folding up almost as fast as banks, and those that survived had few jobs to offer to anyone.

At home, the bottom had fallen out of the chicken business and the fruit would scarcely pay the taxes on our five-acre farm. My father was in the process of becoming an insurance salesman, a tough row to hoe when people have no money. We had plenty to eat, but not much else.

Then one morning, out of the blue, came a telephone call from John Brokenshire, the feisty, red-haired city editor of the *San Jose Mercury Herald*. He had a job to offer. It needed somebody living in the Campbell–Los Gatos–Saratoga area who had some, but not too much, experience as a reporter, and who could serve as a roaming correspondent with little or no supervision. In short, a country reporter.

It was no job for a veteran newshound, who would have been bored stiff; nor for a novice, who would not know where to start; nor for a non-resident, who would not know the area and would have too far to drive every day.

Did I think I was the right man for the job? I certainly did think so. In fact, the job seemed tailor-made for me, and I for it, as it turned out to be.

When I went into San Jose that afternoon to be interviewed, I learned that Brokenshire had kept on file a letter I had written to him six months before to apply for a job. He had not answered the letter, and I had therefore written the *Mercury Herald* off my list as possible employment. But in the interim the previous occupant of the country reporter's job had quit, and Brokenshire somehow remembered my letter among the dozens he had received during that period.

I had been introduced to Brokenshire several years earlier, when as a fringe benefit to winning a college essay contest I had been given a tour of the *Mercury Herald* offices and plant. I think Brokenshire may have been one of the contest judges. In any case, he said he remembered me; whether he did or not, I got the job. In later years we became close friends.

And what a beautiful job that was, especially at that time. I

GHOST TOWNS OF THE Santa Cruz Mountains

By John V. Young
Mercury Herald Staff Writer

An Historical Background of the Santa Clara Valley and Vicinity To Appear Each Sunday in The Mercury Herald

THIS SANTA CRUZ MOUNTAINS feature series will open with an introduction attempting to trace the chief causes and historical significance of the various changes that have affected the region since the days of the Spaniards—the rise and decline of communities, industries and commerce.

BRIEF SKETCHES of some of th- first settlers—"Mountain" Charley McKiernan, "the man with the silver skull;" John Martin Schultheise and the Averill family; the Chases, pioneer millmen, and others, will be followed by stories of the ghost towns of Patchen, Burrell and the community at Summit.

HOW WRIGHT'S STATION came into existence; the story of the railroad; the lumber industry and what happened to it, are told in succeeding installments, together with the histories and recollections of German Town, Loma Prieta, Burrell, Laurel, Glenwood, Alma, Lexington and a score of other towns, villages and gathering places of the period from 1850 to 1910-19.

STORIES OF THE stage coach days, of great forest fires, of the earthquake and floods, and hardship are intermingled with biographical accounts of famous characters that arose in the brief period of the region's affluence.

NO ATTEMPT has been made to prepare a chronological history, but historical references contained in the series are as exact as the memories of the oldest inhabitants, and the incompleteness of records will permit.

HISTORY of the land holdings, particularly of the Mexican grants, which covered almost the entire region, will be traced in some detail, as it forms the basis for many later developments of interest, some of them down to the present day.

SCORES OF OLD PICTURES depicting the region as it once was—a prosperous, thriving center of industry, teeming with people, as compared to its present almost deserted condition, will be shown.

COPIES OF TIN-TYPES of settlers of the '60's and daguerreotypes of the first homesteads to modern photographs of relics of the past—rail fences, hand squared log houses, monuments and landmarks.

MUCH of the material in this series has never before appeared in printed form anywhere. Its collection required weeks of effort, hundreds of miles of travel by automobile over infrequented roads of the mountain district, long hikes afoot over dim trails through forest and brush to find remnants and establish locations of settlements long forgotten, days of searching faded records of the past.

THIS INTERESTING SERIES WILL BEGIN IN THE SUNDAY MERCURY HERALD APRIL 22, AND WILL CONTINUE FOR MANY WEEKS. DON'T MISS A SINGLE ARTICLE. PLACE YOUR SUBSCRIPTION AT ONCE WITH YOUR CARRIER, LOCAL AGENT OR AT THE MAIN OFFICE OF THE

SAN JOSE MERCURY HERALD

30 W. Santa Clara St. Columbia 600

Daily and Sunday

The

San Jose Mercury Herald

Prints the largest and most complete newspaper in Santa Clara County

Full Associated Press reports covering all state, national and world news.

One to two pages of Neighboring Communities news gathered by special correspondents in Santa Clara, San Benito, Santa Cruz and Monterey Counties.

Aunt Polly's Junior Club news for the kiddies.

Farm, Orchard, Garden page edited by Horace G. Keesling.

One to two pages of sports news, club, fraternal, church, and society news and pictures.

Every Sunday a full page of pictures of "The Good Old Days—Here and Elsewhere," reproducing photographs of former times.

Every Monday, a two column feature giving events and comment of 70 years ago taken from the files of the Mercury of that period, and a daily except Monday feature, "Backward Glances"—brief paragraphs of 25 years ago.

"Today Is the Day" a calendar of important events in history.

All these, and other features, combined with the most modern and up to date news gathering facilities have made the Mercury Herald the leading newspaper published in this territory.

Delivered Daily and Sunday
75c Per Month

A full-page advertisement for the author's Sunday feature series "Ghost Towns of the Santa Cruz Mountains." Forty-five years later, the series became a book. (SAN JOSE MERCURY HERALD)

worked my own hours, lived at home, spent the days traveling about talking to old friends. There was just enough excitement on the one hand, and enough difficulty in finding news on the other, to keep me on my toes. I do not recall ever having time to be bored.

The job paid $25 a week, plus another $25 for auto expense. In 1931 that sounded like riches. It kept our family afloat until my father got rolling in the insurance business. Somehow we managed to scrape together the $300 it took to buy the car I had to have for the job. We must have made a good choice, for I drove that 1928 Chevrolet coupe nearly 100,000 miles in the next four years, over all kinds of roads in all kinds of weather.

To some of my acquaintances, my job seemed a bit vague, I realized from their questions. I remember a conversation or two I had with a high school girl who was interested in journalism. She waited for the bus at the main intersection in Los Gatos, where I usually stopped for coffee at the drug store in mid-afternoon.

She asked much about what I did and what I wrote about, and seemed puzzled that it was enough to keep a twenty-four-year old man busy. Either she had more glamorous ideas of newspaper work, or she had no way of knowing what any job paying $25 a week meant in 1933. Later, I had the pleasure of reporting her initial stage triumph in the role of Titania, in a local little theater production of *Midsummer Night's Dream.* She was a shy, pretty child named Olivia De Havilland.

Another Saratoga event comes to mind whenever I think of that country beat, an event of quite a different nature.

Governor Jimmy Rolph, known as "Smiling Jim," was to be guest of honor and principal speaker at a banquet preceding the annual Saratoga Blossom Festival, a lavish extravaganza in the time when it was possible to enjoy a Sunday drive through the prune and apricot orchards without risking life and limb in the traffic.

Having made more than adequate preparation for the ordeal of the banquet, the governor came in on the arm of a husky highway patrolman who had become skilled in the art of supporting un-

The Holy City gas and radio stations (UCSC SPECIAL COLLECTIONS)

steady politicians without appearing to be taking them into custody. For the photographers, however, the pose was not apropos. The patrolman positioned himself behind the governor, but he was too wide for the job. So I was pressed into service. I was not very tall and weighed about 130 pounds with my shoes on. I could easily hide behind the governor and not so easily shore him up until the pictures were shot. After that, I could always say that I had supported Jimmy Rolf for governor, but refrained from doing so.

I encountered the governor once more, in a manner of speaking, a year or two later when I was sent out to Agnew State Hospital to sit out a death watch on him. He was there by chance, having suffered a heart attack while on an official visit.

Since his condition did not permit his being moved, he was attended by a battery of physicians, and died there. I do not remember how long the death watch lasted, but it must have been a matter of days. I learned a lot about poker the hard way from the veteran newsmen on the scene, and after a while I found it hard to distinguish between the members of our bedraggled group and the other guests in the establishment.

I remember quite well the finale of the drama. I was called at midnight by an irate city editor who wanted to know where I had been. The governor had died a couple of hours earlier, he said, and the first word the newspaper had received was over the Associated Press teletype.

It turned out that the head physician had a friend or a brother who worked for the Associated Press in San Francisco and had phoned him to report the governor's demise, quite forgetting about the squad of weary newsmen in the recreation hall. He was a kindly man, I guess, and did not want to interrupt our marathon poker game. I wished he had, for as I recall I was trying to buck a full house with a bobtail flush at the time.

Meanwhile, back on the country beat, I had the daily routine well enough in hand after a couple of years to start looking farther afield for feature material to make up for the scarcity of hard news.

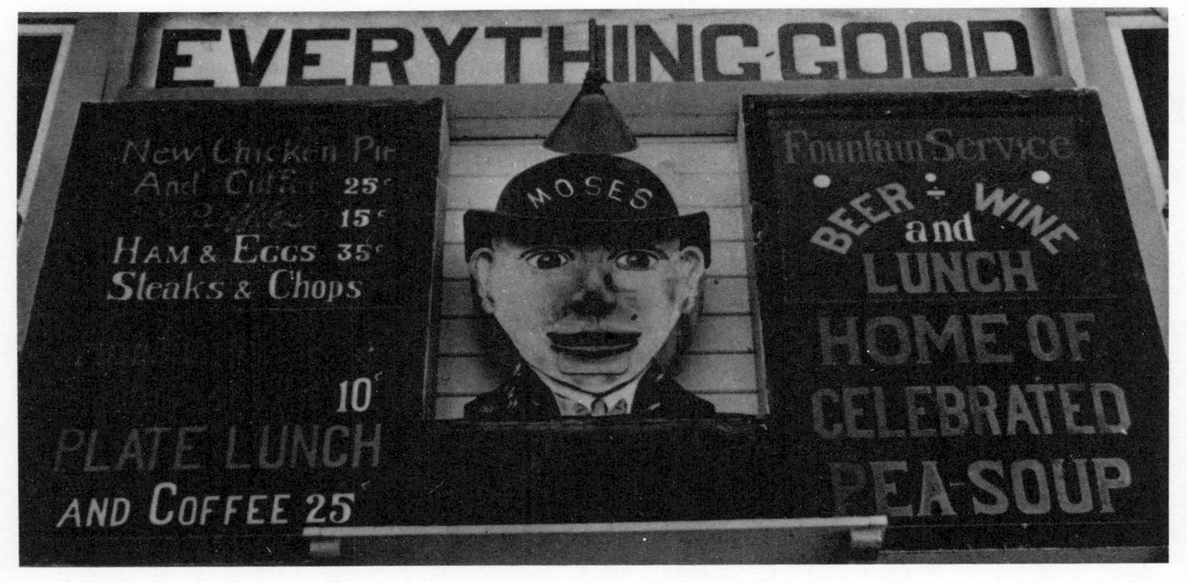

Lunch at Holy City (UCSC SPECIAL COLLECTIONS)

I found it in the adjacent Santa Cruz Mountains, which I had known as a boy. In 1934, I wrote a series of full-page Sunday feature stories called "Ghost Towns of the Santa Cruz Mountains," the product of many interviews with old timers, much digging through faded old family diaries, county histories and back issues of newspapers. The articles were the only newspaper writing I did that survived the years, and are still a prime source of historical material for the region. Forty years later I revised them and they were republished in a book of the same title.

One mountain town that was still thriving in the 1930s, although it has since become a ghost village, was Holy City. It was not affected by Prohibition, as were so many of the mountain towns that depended on the wine industry. It was bone dry in the first place, and its support came almost entirely from tourists, whose numbers were constantly increasing despite the Depression.

Holy City (it was neither holy nor a city) was situated only a few miles south of Los Gatos on what was then the main highway to Santa Cruz (subsequently re-routed to bypass the place). It was founded and run by a self-professed champion of White Supremacy and Prohibition who called himself Father Riker. With a small group of elderly pensioners, he operated a flourishing highway tourist business: restaurant, garage, service station, a bottled-water concession, a radio station of sorts, and a most peculiar newspaper, whereby hangs this tale.

First, some background: During the latter part of Prohibition, which coincided with the early years of the Depression, impecunious newspapermen from the Santa Clara Valley and Monterey Bay area had banded together in what was called "The Fill-the-Hole Club." This so-called club had no bylaws, dues, officers, roster of members or regular meeting place, but it did meet now and then.

The name had two meanings. The first referred to the space left on a newspaper page when the advertising department had finished dummying in the ads for the day. That leftover space, all too glaringly large during the Depression, had to be filled by the editorial staff and was universally known as "The Hole." As may be obvious, the second meaning referred to another gaping void—the gullets of the members, who were thirsty to the last man but rarely able to afford a fancy meal or any beverage stronger than 3.2 beer.

Just for laughs and to fill up space, imaginary accounts of the ficticious good deeds performed by the club appeared from time to time in the newspapers where the members were employed. Thus it was that word of the club reached Father Riker, who fancied himself a newspaperman by virtue of his odd publication called the *Holy City Hurrah.* A full-size, four-page sheet, it was filled entirely with plugs for Holy City enterprises, and editorials and religious homilies, displayed under glaring red-ink headlines. It was, I think, the same material that Father Riker broadcast on Sunday mornings over his tiny radio station, KFQU, which had about the power of a weak light bulb.

Given a little tongue-in-the-cheek encouragement by some members of the club, Father Riker invited the group to a banquet at his mountain restaurant. Obviously, he hoped thereby to be asked to become a member, not having the foggiest idea of the true nature of the organization.

Without stopping to think, if indeed they knew, that Father Riker was a devout teetotaler, the members accepted with glee. On the appointed evening they all showed up at Holy City, not just the dozen or so regulars, but some hard-drinking printers and even some of the business office staff, who ordinarily would not have wanted to be found dead in a gathering of reporters, and vice versa.

If Father Riker was stunned by the size of the crowd—about 30 in all—he did not show it, and perhaps he did not mind. After all, his restaurant was geared to handle whole busloads of people on short notice.

Signs of trouble ahead appeared when the first arrivals tasted the punch, served by Mother Riker from two huge cut-glass bowls on an elaborately decorated side table. The punch had all the authority of a W.C.T.U. afternoon tea.

A hasty conference in a corner took place, and dollar bills were thrust upon two delegates who disappeared up the highway toward a well-known bootlegger's establishment situated conveniently near by. They soon returned, heavily laden. While the rest of the group diverted the attention of the Rikers on the other side of the room, the delegates spiked the punch. They all but nailed it to the table, for the "spiking" consisted of two gallons of white mule—colorless, almost tasteless corn whiskey of lethal strength. Mountain people were said to use it as emergency motor fuel and reported phenomenal performance from their vehicles as a result.

Suitably diluted in the punch, it went down without a whisper, and as stealthily sneaked up on the unwary consumers: namely, the Rikers. The club members worked in relays, offering toasts to everyone they could think of, and of course to be good hosts the Rikers had to chug-a-lug at each toast. It was not long before Mother Riker excused herself and disappeared, and a little later Father Riker floated away to his couch. The party really got going after that, and it lasted a long while. Nobody had told the waiters or kitchen staff when to stop serving. The food was excellent, and something about the mountain air seemed to whet everybody's appetite.

Then someone discovered that Radio Station KFQU was still on the air, Father Riker having turned it on to make some announcement that never came off. The club members took turns singing ribald songs into the microphone, but fortunately the station could not be heard much farther than a mile, if anyone was listening. Next, somebody discovered that there was a long line of urinals in the men's rest room next door, adjoining the service station, equipped to take care of busloads at a time. Over each section of the long facility was a sign that said "STAND CLOSER, PLEASE." At once that became the club slogan, to be shouted in unison whenever anyone stepped up to the microphone to edify the non-audience.

Another discovery was the fact that each of the many flush

toilets in the rest room had a handle labeled "PRESS" on it, and that the handles were easily unscrewed. They soon became the official lapel badges of the club, and for all I know may still be in use as such, being remarkably well-suited for the purpose.

So far as I have ever heard, the club had no response whatever from Father Riker, who apparently decided for some reason that he did not want to become a member after all. Nor did the *Holy City Hurrah* or any other publication to my knowledge ever carry an account of that extraordinary social event, although it had to have been the biggest hurrah in the hamlet's history.

8

FOREST FIRE

I COVERED SEVERAL FOREST FIRES in my years in rural newspaper work, mostly from a respectful distance, but one fire sticks in my mind because I was in the middle of it, and I never want to get that close to one again.

It was during the early 1930s—I do not remember the exact year—while I was covering the country beat for the *San Jose Mercury Herald.* The fire was in the Santa Cruz Mountains and it was a big one. The newspaper wanted a firsthand report and so did the wire services, for the smoke plume could be seen for fifty miles.

As the resident correspondent and nearest reporter to the scene, I was dispatched to do the job. Following directions given to me at the Alma fire station (along with a strong suggestion that I had better stay away from there), I hurried in over obscure, unmarked roads, the smoke and towering flames growing ever closer.

In my haste I made a wrong turn and before I knew it was heading down a canyon directly into the fire. Rounding a sharp bend, I found myself almost surrounded by flames. Bushes were ablaze on both sides of the road; a burning tree was down a few yards in front of my car. I slammed to a stop and roared out backwards as fast as I dared, but not fast enough to keep the heat from cracking the windshield, blistering the paint, and blowing out both front tires. (Fortunately, the car had twenty-one-inch wheels, so flat tires were not so crippling as they would be on a modern car).

Flat tires and all, I backed out of there a quarter mile or so, thanking my lucky stars for a short wheelbase, but very close to panic nevertheless. Barely able to see in the smoky gloom, I finally found a place to turn around and after what seemed an eternity got headed out on the right road. The road led me out on a high, bare, rocky ridge to the fire camp at the end, the site of an abandoned homestead.

An old, tin-roofed farmhouse without windows stood amid a yard full of debris, but at the moment the Waldorf Astoria could not have looked better. Shortly after I arrived, a burning tree closed the road behind me.

Half-a-dozen men and a truck were in the camp, trapped as I was for the moment, but in no danger. The ridge was without trees, and the crew had cleared away what little brush there was around the house. A strong crosswind kept the smoke thinned out, and by the time I got there the main fire had burned its way well below and a good half-mile beyond our ridge top.

The men were keeping the Alma fire station informed by shortwave radio about the progress of the blaze as they could see it. I was permitted to relay a report on my predicament to the newspaper by the same means, but there was too much fire traffic to allow me time to give any details. By the time I got out, rain had quenched the fire and it was all over, so my effort was for naught so far as the news was concerned.

That first night produced a scene out of Dante's Inferno. Now and then the smoke pall would blow aside and we could see the great arc of the fire flaring in the distance. The forest below us had been a tangle of second-growth timber with a dense understory of chaparral, long overdue for burning. Now it was a mass of smouldering embers glowing like fireflies in the dark.

Before I arrived at the camp, the fire had crowned, leaping in giant strides from treetop to treetop, fanned by a stiff wind. Now the constant, menacing moan of the distance fire front sounded like endless lines of freight trains rumbling through the night, now and then punctuated by a sharp report as a big pine or fir exploded.

It was impossible to sleep much and nobody tried. We sat and stared at the fire, listened to the almost constant chatter on the radio, ate sandwiches and drank the cold coffee the fire crew had brought along. We did not talk much.

In retrospect, it seems to me I was out there a week or more, although it could not have been more than a day and a half. Then a bulldozer slogged its way through the burned-over area to make a trail we could use for an escape route. The crew helped me patch up my tires and tubes so I could drive out behind their truck.

Like the rest of the men, I was covered with ashes and soot, bleary-eyed and dispeptic, and I smelled, I am sure, liked a burned hamburger. None of the water we had could have been spared for washing, even if anyone had thought of such a thing.

I recall that I had a battle with the newspaper business office over my expense account for that expedition, and I do not think I won. Since I did not manage to send in a story about the fire, I got little sympathy from the editorial department.

I had nightmares about that trip for quite a while afterward. Even now, after more than forty-five years, I can still see that ring of leaping fire, and hear it, and smell it, as vividly as if it all happened yesterday.

9

BOONDOGGLE IN THE BOONDOCKS

NOT ALL MAPS show it, but a road of sorts joins the wilder parts of Santa Clara and Stanislaus Counties behind Mt. Hamilton, a region virtually unknown to about a million people in and around San Jose, although it lies just over the hills to the east. It is called the Patterson Road because its eastern terminus is in that Stanislaus County town. Over yonder it hooks up with the rough but much older and better known (but still seldom-travelled) shunpike from Mt. Hamilton to Livermore.

I have not been over the Patterson Road in nearly half a century, and then was over it only once, before the western half of it was any road at all. I rather doubt that it is used much now except by an occasional rancher, hunter, game warden or fire fighter. Nature lovers no doubt use it to see the spring wildflowers. On some road maps it appears as a thin, wiggly blue line, meaning that it is an established route but not much more, graded in election years, usually passable. Beyond that I would not want to be responsible for sending anyone over it, as I was once with dire results.

That was the time I piloted what must have been the first motor vehicle ever to traverse that particular piece of rugged terrain in the back of beyond, in company with a county official who also should have known better. It was back in the early 1930s, before the days of four-wheel-drive vehicles, when off-the-road exploration called for a lot more ingenuity and determination than present-day all-terrain vehicles require under most circumstances.

The idea for the trip came from Max Watson, at the time Santa Clara County's juvenile probation officer. Max had just achieved local fame by cornering the teazel market, but that is another story. Max came to me, as I recall, because I was then writing occasional travel stories for the *San Jose Mercury Herald,* reporting on out-of-the-way places of interest to Sunday drivers who didn't mind a few bumps.

Max was interested in finding out whether it might be possible to drive a car over the Cerro Colorado range behind Mt. Hamilton, not just for a lark but to try to establish a short truck route between the San Joaquin Valley and San Jose. He thought such a route might lure a lot of profitable truck traffic away from the two existing routes, both much longer: Pacheco Pass via Gilroy to the south, and Altamont Pass via Livermore to the north. On paper it looked like a good idea.

Equipped with food, water, sleeping bags (just in case), an axe, shovel, chains, rope, and spare tires, Max and I started out just after dawn one late spring morning. I was driving my trusty old 1928 Chevrolet coupe, counting on its twenty-one-inch wheels to get us over rough spots.

We chugged up and over Mt. Hamilton, passed Lick Observatory, and wound down the other side on the back road to Livermore, then not much more than a dirt track. Somewhere after we reached the bottom of the long grade at the headwaters of Isabel Creek, we started looking for and eventually found a dim ranch track that led off to the east. It appeared to be a way to reach the top of the Cerro Colorado range looming on the horizon ahead of us.

The author atop Castle Rock in the Santa Cruz Mountains (YOUNG)

We were a bit nervous, I recall, not wanting to be mistaken for revenuers in a country reputed to be the hangout of moonshiners. But we saw no one, and the ranch road petered out at an abandoned homestead in front of an old corral. We had no choice but to take to the hills, literally, for there was not even a wheel track or a hoof print beyond the corral.

Of course, the way was rough and slow, but aside from having to dig a long, shallow furrow to keep us from slipping sidewise down one steep, grassy hillside, we had no particular difficulty until we gained the top of the ridge. It was then about noon. Wide and comparatively flat, the ridge was covered with small boulders and a dense stand of dead trees, scrub oak and pinon evidently killed off by a fire or drought years before. The stuff was rotten to such an extent we found we could bash our way through like a tank, pushing down the smaller trees with the front bumper.

Eventually, we battered our way to the ruins of a quicksilver mine, a welcome sight as it gave us our first positive reference point on our topographic map. We were, the map said, a little north of Mt. Stakes, elevation 3808 feet, just where we had wanted to be. About all that was left of the works was about half an acre of broken bricks and the remains of a smelter and its tall smokestack.

Leaving the car, we walked around the ruins, keeping an eye out for rattlesnakes and wondering what had become of the road that must have led to the mine at one time. Presently, we saw a road, well below us on the Patterson side, at the bottom of a steep hill. We scrambled down to find, to our surprise, a modern, well-graded gravel road with steel culverts, running up and down the canyon. It seemed to have no connection, however, with the mine back up the hill a hundred feet above. Lacking wings, we appeared to be high and dry.

A little further scouting revealed that the brick chimney at the mine had fallen down the hillside almost to the road, providing a very rough but possibly passable route at an angle of perhaps thirty degrees. It was fairly simple for us to shovel away the bank to make it possible for the car to slide down the last ten feet to the road, if we could get it that far.

Well, we did. We tied one end of our tow rope to the bumper and took a couple of turns around a tree with the other end. While Max paid out the rope, I drove with the door open and one foot on the running board in case I had to bail out in a hurry. Wheels locked, the car slid and slithered and banged over the bricks and crashed down onto the road, and we were there in one piece. We gave the car a thorough examination but found no damage worse than a few new dents in the gas tank.

We then drove up the canyon to see where the road went, wondering if we had somehow missed a new route over the range. We need not have worried, for the road stopped abruptly at the County line, not far from where we had crossed the ridge. The line was marked by a brand-new Stanislaus County road sign. On the Santa Clara County side there was nothing at all but wilderness.

Next we turned around and drove down the canyon, toward Patterson. A mile or two down the road, we rounded a bend to find some sort of celebration in full swing in the middle of the road. In fact, the entire road was taken up with tables loaded with food, some suspicious-looking jugs, a portable barbecue pit, a speaker's stand, and a very energetic three-piece cowboy combo. There were lots of people, I guessed a hundred or so, many of whom seemed to be well into the spirit of the occasion.

Everything stopped dead as we came into view, even the racket the band was making. Absolute amazement was written on the faces of everyone present, for they all knew perfectly well that the road whence we had come did not go anywhere. As we came to a halt, we were besieged by questions, everyone talking at once.

After a while we got things straightened out to everyone's satisfaction, including our own. The picnic, we learned, was to celebrate the opening of a new Stanislaus County prison farm down the road a piece. One of the farm's first projects had been the building of the new road to the county line.

Then we learned that the Stanislaus County supervisors had invited the Santa Clara County supervisors to attend the dedication, evidently sharing Max Watson's idea of a new road between the two neighbors, but had received no response.

Thus Max and I unwittingly became Santa Clara County's ambassadors without portfolio. Max let it be known that he had planned the trip that way as a surprise, and maybe he had, but at the time I had a strong feeling he was as surprised as anyone else, or as I was. (Later, I found what the catch was. We had ignored the fact that the reigning head of the Santa Clara County board of supervisors owned a good part of Gilroy and he was not about to encourage the development of a competing route.)

I took some pictures and promised to give the project some publicity, which I soon did in the form of a Sunday road feature. Despite the fact that I emphasized the terrors of the trip, pointing out that the Santa Clara County portion of the route was strictly for mountain goats and no place at all for Sunday drivers in Cadillacs, a lot of them tried it.

My first intimation of trouble came from an irate forest ranger, who stormed into the office to complain he had spent all the previous weekend with a team of horses hauling mired flatlanders out of the mud behind Mt. Hamilton where he was stationed. He wanted the traffic stopped, somehow.

It seems that Max and I had cut up the grassy hillsides pretty badly on our pioneering trip. When it rained a few days later, and the first cars tried to follow our obvious route, they made it worse. In fact, they made it impassable.

I tried. I wrote another story describing the situation and warning the public that nobody should even think of trying to go that way, but the article only seemed to inflame the populace. I guess it was a month or so before heavy rain, or the ranger, or both, finally blocked the road entirely, or the novelty wore off.

Nothing came of the Patterson project for a long time. I do not know when the present road was built, or how, or why, since it happened long after I left the region. But it is on the map, although I doubt that it is used much by heavy trucks or is apt to be unless, they build a tunnel under Mt. Hamilton some day.

Some day I hope to navigate that road anyhow and see if I can remember any of the route. For all I know, that old quicksilver mine might even have been in operation in the interim, during one of the periods when mercury prices have soared. In any case, according to the map, the Stanislaus County prison farm is still there. (Friends tell me that the road now carries quite a bit of traffic.)

10

ST. JAMES PARK

LEST IT APPEAR that life for a small town newspaperman in the 1930s was all thin beer and skittles, I feel obliged to report on the grimmest episode in which, as a reporter, I ever had any part, however minor. It gave me nightmares for years.

Coming out of a movie in San Jose the night of November 26, 1933, I heard a strange and frightening roar in the distance, a kind of keening that stirred a primeval tingling on the back of my neck. I had no idea what it was until I saw the people running down First Street toward the north and I overheard something about a lynching.

Then I knew at once what was happening, although I had missed the earlier radio newscasts that later were blamed for the massed turnout of citizens. Evidently they had started gathering much earlier in the day, but did not become a mob until well after dark, in the manner of mobs.

Never before had I heard the hideous roar of a mob in full cry and I never want to hear it again. In fact, if I ever do hear it again or anything like it, I shall run the other way as fast as I can

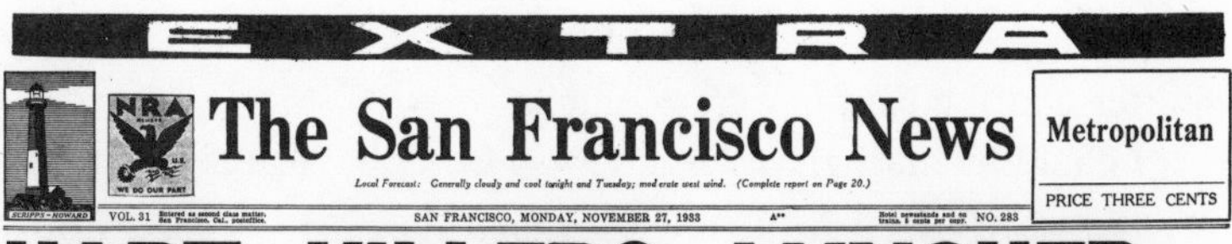

EXTRA

The San Francisco News

Metropolitan

Local Forecast: Generally cloudy and cool tonight and Tuesday; moderate west wind. (Complete report on Page 20.)

PRICE THREE CENTS

VOL. 31 Entered as second class matter, San Francisco, Cal., postoffice. SAN FRANCISCO, MONDAY, NOVEMBER 27, 1933 A** Hotel newsstands and on trains, 5 cents per copy. NO. 283

HART KILLERS LYNCHED; MOB MEMBERS ESCAPE

FINDING OF BODY STARTS RIOT

BATTERING RAM AT WORK -:- KIDNAPERS MOBBED

BATTERING DOWN THE JAIL DOOR. NOTE THE TEAR GAS CLOUDS. PHOTO BY MELVIN B. MEACHAM.

DRAGGING THURMOND AND HOLMES TO THEIR DEATH. THE MOB IS BEATING THEM. PHOTO BY EDDIE MURPHY.

JAIL STORMED, PAIR HANGED ON PARK TREES; EIGHT INJURED

BY RICHARD V. HYER
The News Staff Correspondent

SAN JOSE, Nov. 27:—The mortal remains of Brooke L. Hart and the two men who kidnaped and murdered him lay side by side today in the coroner's morgue.

The confessed slayers, Thomas H. Thurmond and John M. Holmes, were lynched amid the approving roars of 5000 infuriated men and women shortly before town bells tolled the Sabbath midnight.

Identity of the mob leaders who stormed the jail in the face of clouds of tear gas remained unknown.

Deputy sheriffs and police, themselves blinded by the fumes, said they could not see anyone and recognized no one.

Thurmond was lynched at 11:20 p m and Holmes followed him to eternity at rope's end five minutes later. They met death in St. James Park, directly across First st. from the county jail and courthouse.

Since midmorning men and women, many of them with lunch baskets and children, had gathered under the trees.

All San Jose had known, it became apparent today from the moment word sped through the city that young Hart's body had been found, that lynch law was to be invoked at 11 p m.

Mob violence exploded at about 8 o'clock when Depuy Sheriff Joseph Walsh, whether intentionally was not known, loosed a tear gas bomb in front of the hundreds packed before the jail. Deputy John Moore followed it with another grenade.

For the next three hours a pitched battle raged, but deputies and police, who carried small arms and riot guns, did not fire a shot.

Sheriff William J. Emig and two of his deputies, John Moore and Howard Buffington, the only officers who had keys to the cells, were beaten and mauled, the sheriff and Deputy Buffington seriously. They were taken to the San Jose Hospital.

Lynching Had Been Planned

As 20 men, many of them of youthful appearance, fought their way into the ancient red brick structure, some of the leaders claimed they were Santa Clara University students.

That the lynching was long-planned was evident.

Coroner Amos Williams received, at 6 p m, a telephone call which instructed him to be in St. James Park at 11 o'clock for the bodies of Thurmond and Holmes.

The coroner, failing to learn the identity of the speaker, paid no attention to the message.

Word that young Hart's body had been recovered was received by Sheriff Emig at 10 a m. From then until the two killers, shrieking futile protestations of mistaken identity, were dragged to the little park, events moved with terrible swiftness.

Sheriff Emig at once summoned Charles O'Brien jr, young Hart's closest friend, to go to the spot on the Hayward shore where two duck hunters had found the body. Mr. O'Brien was to make positive identification.

Jail Defenders Organized

When they departed Undersheriff Earle G. Hamilton began organization of all forces to defend the jail and save the prisoners from mob violence.

A sheriff's truck was parked across the alley leading from the jail to First st. On the Julian st. side a big sedan was placed in a similar position.

At the undersheriff's request Police Chief J. N. Black sent 20 officers and a patrol wagon loaded with steel "horses," used for barricading streets and planks.

These were erected as blockades in front of the truck and sedan, closing off the two lanes leading to the jail. Five officers were stationed in the sheriff's private office facing the steel door at the main jail entrance. They were armed with tear gas bombs.

Meanwhile, word young Hart's body had been found swept through the city. Before the extra editions of local newspapers were being screamed on the streets, throngs were beginning to converge on the jail.

People Are Orderly at First

For the first few hours the people were orderly. There were no overt actions. But there was a grim deadly undertone.

At 5 p m Sheriff Emig and Mr. O'Brien returned from their tragic errand. The slain youth's body had been identified.

The crowd, more frightening in its quiet orderliness than a mob in disorder, caused the sheriff to make an appeal for help to E. Raymond Cato, chief of the State Highway Patrol.

Mr. Cato was a guest at the ranch of Louis Oneal, Santa Clara county political dictator, from whose office the capture and confessions of Thurmond and Holmes were first announced.

Following the call to Mr. Cato, Capt. Walter McGrory of the County

(Turn to Page 8, Column 1)

Lynching headlines from the San Francisco News, November 27, 1933.

go. That's what I should have done that night, had I but known what was waiting for me in St. James Park—but I was a young reporter and the alarms were sounding.

I could no more have turned away from that awful scene than I could have ignored a hotel fire or an airplane crash in the street.

This is what was happening: A young man named Brooke Hart, son of a prominent local merchant, had been kidnapped and then murdered by a pair of unemployed local layabouts. The FBI caught the two men (Thomas Thurmond and Jack Holmes) and lodged them in the county jail, where they were said to have confessed.

The failure to move them well out of town was a mistake, for public indignation already was running high and the machos were thumping their beer mugs on the bars in the local bistros and telling themselves there ought to be a necktie party. Perhaps nothing but tough talk would have resulted except that the talk reached the ears of a popular radio newscaster who put it on the air as an event in progress. People turned out en masse to watch the sport and soon were caught up in the savage hysteria that pervaded the streets like a lethal fog.

I have heard estimates about the size of the mob ranging from a few hundred to several thousand. To me it looked like a frightful number of presumably decent citizens turned into a pack of hyenas. They were all kinds—well-dressed businessmen and housewives, students, bums from the slums, professional people, people of all races and nationalities, a cross-section of the city to its everlasting shame.

The street was too jammed for me to try to drive, so I ran with the mob the half-dozen blocks to the scene of the action. By the time I arrived it was almost all over but the shouting, which was growing in ever-increasing volume.

People were milling about making ugly noises in their throats, like wild animals worrying a bone, a wordless, chilling sound like nothing uttered by humans. As I arrived, a large knot of the participants surged into the park and the drama went into its final act to the accompaniment of a new crescendo in the noise of the mob.

Later I learned the details of the earlier action from Bob Couchman, another *Mercury* scribe, who had locked himself inside a jail office and was telephoning in his eyewitness account of the happenings there. The mob had used a large steel pipe to smash down the jailhouse door, swept aside the token resistance of the jailers and deputies, ignored a cloud of tear gas, and had seized and savagely battered the two kidnappers in their cells.

Thurmond was already unconscious—or dead—from a blow on the head, but Holmes fought like a fiend all the way when the mob hauled the pair across the street to a hanging tree in St. James Park, which is where I first saw them. His hands untied, Holmes tried to climb the rope they put around his neck, but the mob yanked him down by the heels and the fall evidently broke his neck, for he quit his kicking and screaming abruptly. Then the mob went entirely berserk.

I saw people tear the shoes and then the soiled trousers off the victims and rip them up for souvenirs.

I saw a clergyman vainly try to stop the mob by holding up his arms and pleading for mercy. He was nearly knocked down and trampled by the mob for his pains.

I saw a man try to set fire to the dangling feet of the victims with a cigarette lighter.

I saw women and children flailing at the bodies with sticks.

I saw mothers holding up small children for a better view.

I saw a prominent attorney—an officer of the court of justice—on crutches, struggling to get a place on the ropes.

I saw people spitting on the bodies. I saw people vomiting, crying, wringing their hands, and there was pungent evidence of incontinence.

And I saw a woman beating on a tree with her fists and moaning, "Oh dear God! No! No! No! No!"

I saw other things I never want to see again, things I can never forget—saw them and heard them and smelled them. The park was a veritable jungle that night, and the air was rank with blood lust.

I wondered then as I wonder now how any of those hordes of temporary lunatics managed to sleep that night or to face their families and their fellows the next day. I do not think I felt any pity for the kidnappers, but rather for the participants, if I felt anything but horror.

Still trying to maintain some semblance of reportorial detachment, I took in all that I could stand to see and hear and then ran to the office. Amid the pandemonium of conflicting reports and the jangle of a dozen phones all ringing at once, I recited my impressions to a rewrite man who wove them into one of the several articles the newspaper was preparing. I was not alone—several other off-duty men were unable to stay away and came in to contribute their two bit's worth.

At the time, I did not have a flash camera and would have been too frightened to use it if I had. Not so timid was Loris Gardner, the *Mercury Herald's* intrepid chief photographer. He made a classic shot of the mob charging the jailhouse door with its battering ram. His close-up flash lit the scene as if a searchlight had been turned on it. I do not know to this day how Loris and his camera got away unscathed, but the photo, in merciless detail, was on the front page of the newspaper the next morning. Later, it appeared in several magazines.

I think a San Francisco reporter won the Pulitzer Prize for his coverage of that terrible event. The *Mercury Herald* did not win any prizes but that left no regrets I know of on the part of the staff. That story was much too close to home for comfort or for any extremes of journalistic objectivity.

Rumors ran around the city for days or weeks, and for days or weeks the curious came in droves to drive around the jail and the park to view the scene of the action. The rumors had it that the whole sorry business was a put-up job that had backfired; that the two men were merely stooges and not the brains behind the kidnapping; that the affair had been staged to keep the men from talking in court; that a squadron of highway patrolmen had been held a couple of blocks away all during the lynching, etc., etc., ad nauseum. I do not remember whether any of these stories were ever printed locally but I doubt it, since this was before the days of mass-circulation scandal sheets in San Jose.

Plenty did get printed there and elsewhere—editorials and letters deploring the state of affairs; threats by various police officials about impending mass indictments and arrests; an unfortunate remark by Governor James Rolph lauding the lynching; news about numerous inquiries and investigations on how it all had been allowed to happen, and why the sea was boiling hot and whether pigs had wings. So far as I can recall, nothing whatever came of any of it.

It took a long time for the tattered trees of St. James Park to grow new limbs and at least one—that one—had to be cut down, just as the hapless guests of honor were cut down by the police after the tumult and the shouting had died away and the members of the mob had changed back into citizens and gone home.

It was California's last recorded lynching.

11

CAT HOUSE CRASH

OUR ABILITY to print the news in those days of the old *Mercury Herald* was limited as much by our own interpretation of the mores of the period as it was by the newspaper's policies. It now seems as if we were then only just emerging from the restrictions and hypocricies of the Victorian era. I recall our talented staff artist, Jimmy Glynn, having to paint in some knee-length underpants on a much-too-candid low-angle photo of a drum majorette in order to render it suitable for a nice family newspaper.

We encountered one news story that severely taxed our collective talents in the art of euphemism. It started with a report of a small-plane accident at the local airport, where an inexperienced pilot had managed to trip his landing gear on a power line and had landed upside down on the tarmac. He was not badly hurt but his plane was, and the FAA or whatever agency was in charge of such matters at the time went out to investigate.

Then it all come out. The plane had been landing in a forbidden direction, but why? Well, the investigators finally succeeded in turning up the fact that just beyond the airport and the power line was a three-story house with a tin roof. It was indeed a house, euphemistically speaking. In fact, it was a house of ill repute run by a popular lady known as Rosie.

Sunday fliers at the airport had often noticed, and discussed among themselves in ribald fashion, the arrival and departure of automobiles at frequent intervals in front of the house. They even timed the intervals. Armed with this precise data, they took turns buzzing the tin roof of the establishment, and then laughed themselves silly speculating on just how precise their timing might have been and the impact of the buzzing. That was what happened to the unfortunate flier who tripped over the power wire. He was not trying to land, merely attempting to pull out of a power dive over the roof.

I remember quite well the agonies we went through trying to tell what happened that day, in language we were able to print, and I am not at all sure we succeeded, or what we did about the heading.

Nowadays it would be no problem. The story, slugged CAT HOUSE CRASH, would leave little to the imagination, except perhaps for the unknown details of what took place up there on the third floor. It might even be illustrated with a cartoon.

12

FREMONT'S PEAK

I LEFT the *Mercury Herald* early in 1935 in search of greener pastures and spent the next two years on other small-town newspapers. Since I put in more than half of that time on Salinas newspapers, I think of the period as my Salinas years. Although the time was actually quite short, it was often hectic, as the following episode will illustrate.

During a brief stint on the old *Salinas Morning Post* in 1936, I became interested in early County history and did a lot of reading on the subject. Some of what I read did not square with the legend behind a popular annual event celebrated by the Native Sons & Daughters of the Golden West on top of a high peak in the County.

Now a state park, the peak was named for the famous pathfinder, Captain John C. Fremont, who had guided a so-called topographic expedition through California in 1846. A highly controversial figure, Fremont undoubtedly was an agent provocateur engaged in quasi-official activities designed to stir up trouble with Mexico as an excuse for the Mexican War.

At the time of his visit to the peak, he was in a hurry. Hot

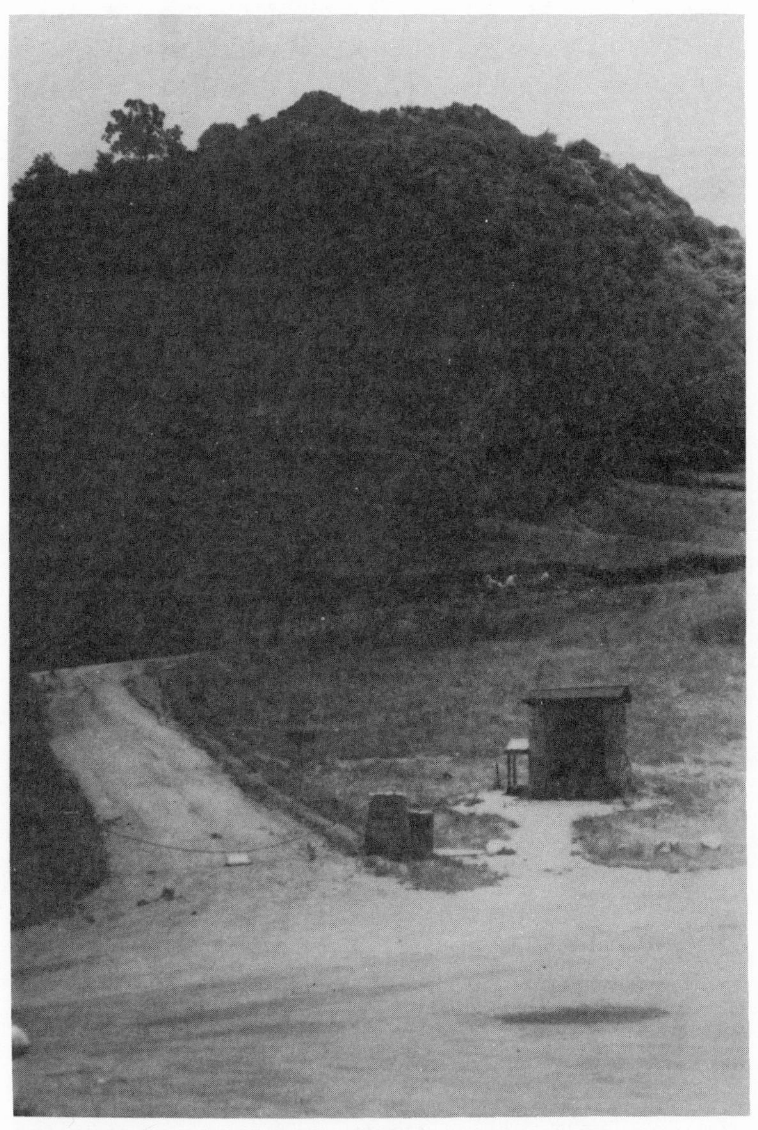

So-called Fremont's Peak (UCSC SPECIAL COLLECTIONS)

on his trail was a Mexican general with a small regiment of soldiers. The Mexican general had a good idea of what Fremont was up to and had a calaboose in Mexico City in mind for the Yankee invaders.

According to the popular legend, Fremont and his men took refuge on top of the peak and valiantly fought off attack after attack by the Mexican army, before finally escaping one night. In neighboring San Juan Bautista, gullible visitors used to be shown a pile of cannonballs alleged to have rolled down the mountainside during the pitched battle. Local artists turned out sketches purporting to illustrate the celebrated event.

The only problem was that as a matter of historical record there never was a battle of Fremont Peak. Not a shot was fired on either side. According to my reading of the data, Fremont did retreat up the peak, where he and his men built a log fort and some huge bonfires from the abundant ponderosa pines that fringed the top.

Down below, the Mexicans maintained a discreet distance, for while they outnumbered the Americans five or ten to one, they all were armed with smooth-bore muskets. The Americans, on the other hand, were equipped with Kentucky long rifles, with which they were said to be able to shoot the eye out of a prairie dog at a hundred yards, more or less. In an earlier encounter in southern California, these same twenty-five long-riflemen were reported to have amused themselves by shooting the buttons off the uniforms of the Mexican soldiers when they got too close.

So the Mexican general waited three or four days until the fires died down on the mountain top, then sent scouts to climb the peak. They found not a soul there—by that time Fremont and his band were half way to Oregon.

All this I duly reported in the *Salinas Morning Post* on the occasion of the annual celebration of the Battle of Fremont's Peak. The story cost the struggling little morning newspaper about 150 subscribers—presumably the entire membership of the N. S. & D. of the G. W.—a number it could ill afford to lose.

The letters and phone calls we received were far from complimentary, and some were surprisingly violent coming from elderly people. None agreed with my version of the event, but neither did anyone offer any documented rebuttal. The fairly large population of residents of Mexican descent didn't like the story much either.

The editor, no history buff himself, strongly urged me to confine my efforts to current (non-controversial) news and leave history debunking to historians. I think the only reason he didn't fire me was because he had let the story slip by him, and he should have known better even if I did not.

So much for investigative reporting in the 1930s.

13

FIRST CAR DOWN THE BIG SUR HIGHWAY

IT WAS ALSO while I was working as a reporter on the *Salinas Morning Post* that I had another bright idea that almost cost me my job. That it did not was only because an enterprising auto dealer had a lively imagination and a sense of humor, rare in the business.

For some reason not now entirely clear, I undertook to revive an almost forgotten newspaper feature known as the Sunday autologue, which probably will not be remembered now by anyone much under fifty. I think I did it partly to earn Brownie points, partly to wangle a shiny new car and a tank full of fuel to take some friends on a long Sunday outing at no cost. In any event, so long as I was willing to donate my time, my boss thought it was a fine idea. So did the local auto dealers. So did I, the first two or three times.

In case you do not remember them, Sunday autologues were common to metropolitan newspapers in the 1920s, when motor touring was still novel enough to support full-time automotive editors and special sections in the papers devoted exclusively to automotive news. Actually, they were elaborate blurbs in which the alleged virtues of various makes of cars were extolled at length.

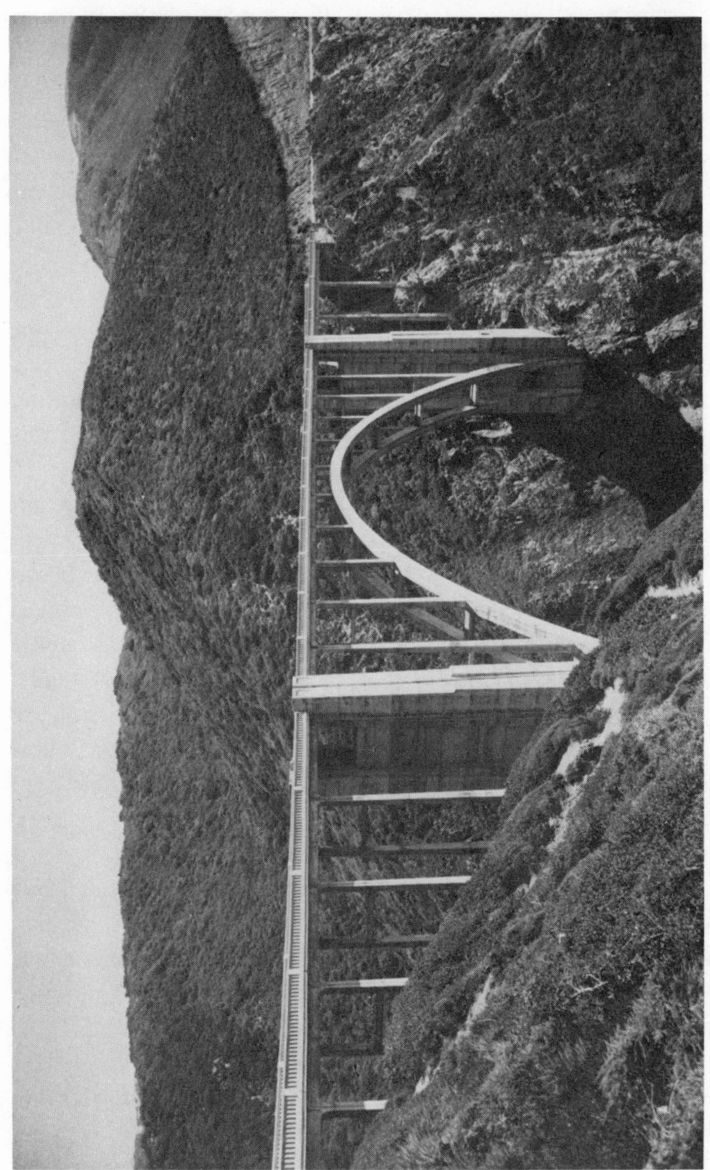

One of the spectacular "rainbow bridges" along the Big Sur highway. (YOUNG)

Full-page spreads showed the car of the week at its best advantage, pictured under flowering trees, reflected in still pools, or climbing impossible grades at angles enhanced by tilting the camera.

Invariably a bevy of smiling beauties, attired to suit the season, adorned the scene and hid some of the car's uglier features. A map showed the reader how to get to whatever scenic wonders the story mentioned. The maps often were works of art, decorated with cute cartoons in the blank areas. Those were the days.

The theory of the autologue seemed to be that such largess on the part of the newspaper must arouse automobile advertising directors to a frenzy of space buying, along with purveyors of accessories, tires, gas, oil, and spark plugs. I guess it worked, back in the days of innocence and auto clubs, before the Federal Trade Commission began to read ads.

Now back to Salinas. I chose one Sunday to try a totally untravelled route for which (in retrospect) a tank or a tractor might have been better suited than a brand new Chevrolet sedan. It was the as-yet uncompleted ninety-three-mile stretch of the now-famous Carmel–San Simeon highway, California's fabulously scenic Route 1, more often now known simply as the Big Sur highway. Actually, the new highway started at Big Sur. From there on it was closed and guarded during the eighteen years required to build it at a cost of more than ten million dollars. Since no contractor in his right mind would tackle the job back then, it was built with convict labor. Men with rifles patrolled the route.

It took some political muscle to get permission to drive through with a passenger car, without a doubt the first civilian vehicle ever to do so, but in those days even small-town newspapers still had muscle. Anyhow, it was a Republican newspaper during a Republican year in the statehouse.

So, with lunches provided by the two young ladies we brought along strictly for pictorial purposes, four of us started out in a shiny new Chevvy, heading down the coast. It was relatively easy going until we got past Big Sur, where the old road ended. Right off the bat we met up with one of those incredible rainbow arch bridges for which the route was to become famous. The trouble was, the rainbow arch was not quite finished. It had a gap in the middle. We had no choice but to slither down a muddy trail to the bottom of the gorge, whence we were dragged ignominiously up the other side by a bulldozer.

We did this several times, and each time the car suffered visibly. Farther on, our once-shiny sedan underwent showers of gravel and mud, bombardment by small boulders from fresh side-hill slashes, and a couple of times minor encounters with house-sized rocks in the middle of the so-called road. But somehow we reached the other end, twelve or fourteen hours later. One head-light was broken, the windshield was cracked, and the body showed innumerable dents. The car looked like it had been to war rather than on a pleasant Sunday outing. We limped back to Salinas by the main valley highway, in time to snatch a few hours sleep before going to work.

The car looked even worse in the cold gray light of dawn, but I had no choice except to take it back to the dealer and hope for the best. I envisioned a bill for several hundred dollars in repairs, which I did not have, or the summary conclusion of my job, or both.

To my amazement and delight, the dealer was as pleased as I had been dismayed. Far from being concerned over the sorry condition of the vehicle, he put it in his show window just as it was. He plastered the window with pictures I provided, plus some of his own, along with a printed text. According to his telling, the car had proved itself to be as rugged as a World War I tank, as comfortable under adverse conditions as a harem couch, as economical to run as a bicycle, etc., etc. I think he was secretly astonished (as I was) that the car ever made it home at all.

All I had to do then was to write the autologue to fit his prescription, which I felt obliged to do since the little matter of my job was at stake. Somehow, I did not manage to make any more autologues after that.

14

THE MISPLACED BEAR

ONE LITTLE INCIDENT from my Salinas newspaper days sticks in my mind as about the funniest story I ever handled, one that made the front page of newspapers all over the country.

An elderly ranch hand went out one Sunday to shoot rabbits for the pot in the foothills of the Santa Lucia range west of King City, then a sleepy little farm town in the upper Salinas Valley. He was quite evidently well fortified with wine, so much so that when he came up over a low hill and found himself face to face with a bear, he up and fired his .22 rifle at point-blank range. Had he been sober, he doubtless would have dropped the gun and taken to his heels without waiting to shoot, for full-grown bears are notably hard to kill and when wounded become exceedingly irritable.

Even for a marksman, shooting a bear with a .22 rifle would be sheer madness, or suicidal; but this hunter was a very lucky man. His shot from the hip went in between the bear's eyes, in about the only vulnerable spot in its skull, and dumdummed in the animal's brain. The bear dropped dead in its tracks.

Suddenly sobered, the man ran all the way back to King City.

Unable to find a game warden, he gasped out his story to a state highway patrolman he met. The patrolman took him to the local justice of the peace. The patrolman and the justice were both aware there had been no bears in those mountains for nearly half a century and one horrid possibility came quickly to their minds—that the ranch hand had shot a man, maybe a Russian who walked like a bear.

Hastily they organized a posse, rounded up a doctor and a stretcher, and hurried back to the scene of the shooting, guided to some extent by the shooter. There they found the bear all right, a full-grown sow, dead as a doornail, shot smack between the eyes.

That much was a relief, but a considerable flurry resulted. First, what to do with the shooter? The answer to that was easy. As there was no open season on bears, no any closed season either, he was released with a stern admonition not to pull the trigger until he could see the whites of the target's eyes.

But second, where did the bear come from? For a few days rumors flew about the hills and valleys, rumors of missing cattle and unidentified raids on hog pens, and ranchers kept a shotgun handy when they went to bed.

Then, after the event had been widely publicized in the press and on the radio, a shamefaced National Park Service official provided the answer.

The bear was a rogue from Yosemite. Fed daily on garbage and tourist marshmallows, it had become a dangerous nuisance in the campground and had been trapped. Then it had been surreptitiously removed to the Coast Range west of King City, perhaps on the theory that the region needed some bears—well, at least one bear.

I often wondered who got the bear skin for a rug.

15

FUDGE BONUSES AND UNIONS

THE REWARDS of small-town journalism in the 1930s were meager enough, financially speaking, but nothing in my experience ever quite approached the payoff for weeks of extra work on the old *Salinas Index-Journal* (now the *Salinas Californian*).

The big event in Salinas in 1936 was, and presumably still is, the annual rodeo. Besides bringing in a lot of outside cash to the town's merchants, it was a great boost to the newspaper's advertising income. As was (and still is) the custom in small-town newspapers, the advertising department went all out to sell enough ads to fill a huge special rodeo edition, many times the size of the ordinary weekend issue. I will not go into the high pressure tactics used to sell the ads. I do know that for every full-page ad, a dozen of lesser size came in, leaving a lot of odd space to be filled by the editorial staff.

The extra copy meant extra hours, since the editorial staff was never any larger than the bare minimum needed to get out the daily paper. Extra hours meant late afternoons, evenings, and weekends spent excavating and writing column after column of stuff we on the editorial side were convinced nobody would ever read.

We warmed up ancient legends and historical anecdotes dating from Spanish times, scoured the countryside for agricultural oddities, made life miserable for the town's librarians, dug back through previous special editions for material we hoped nobody would remember (assuming that anyone had read those editions either).

Fortunately, the details are dim now. I do not remember whether we worked two weeks or two months of extra time on that edition. The union printers in the back shop did not make life any easier for us, reminding us on every possible occasion that they were raking in more on overtime alone than any of us were making in total salary. Their base wage was twice ours to begin with. But overtime pay for editorial workers before the Guild? You would have to be kidding. We were going to get our reward in Heaven, or just perhaps we would get some sort of bonus, we thought.

Sure enough, on the Saturday afternoon the special edition went to press, a monstrosity of forty-eight or sixty-four pages or some such, we were told to stick around a little while—the boss had something for us. The boss—a pleasant young man we hardly knew—came in and made a nice speech, full of praise for our sterling efforts, commendation for the excellence of our product (I'd bet a buck he never read a word of it), and more of same.

"And now," he said with a flourish, "as a token of our appreciation . . ." and he stepped aside to admit his wife, who was waiting in the wings with a box.

Holding onto the box, she walked it around the room. It was homemade fudge. It was a big box—there must have been at least two pieces in it for each of us. (Do not think those things didn't happen in the 1930s. They still happen. In recent times, I have been told, the publisher of the *Santa Fe New Mexican* brought in a box of apples from his ranch to hand out to the editorial staff as a reward for a quite similar occasion.)

I rather imagine almost any small-town newspaperman could report a similar experience. I always did maintain that a sense of humor was an even more essential requirement for a rural journalist than a sense of news or the ability to spell.

I mentioned in passing the Guild—the American Newspaper Guild—the union of editorial and business office employees organized in the mid-1930s but not really effective until the following decade.

For background, remember that the National Labor Relations Act (called the Wagner Labor Act) was passed by Congress and signed into law as a New Deal action in 1935. It was not until 1937, however, that it was upheld by the Supreme Court, on a suit brought by the Guild in defense of a San Francisco newspaper reporter who had been fired for Guild activity. It became known as the Burgess case.

In 1936, however, I knew or cared about as much about the Guild as I did about Sanskrit theology. Obviously, it was going to be a long time reaching Salinas, if it ever did. What I did not know then was that small-town newspaper proprietors from coast to coast were jittery as a bunch of Mexican jumping beans about the Wagner Labor Act and its possible impact on their non-union employees. There loomed the horrid prospect that the Guild might even invade the editorial department, and legally.

In that same year—1936—that we put out that special edition in Salinas, the city had just undergone a nearly catastrophic strike of lettuce workers. (See the next chapter.) Long before the days of Caesar Chavez, the lettuce workers were making their first determined stand for more money. They were being called Communists as a result. John Steinbeck was living there then. (I interviewed him once, but for some unaccountable reason, the paper did not print the interview.) He gave his famous definition of a Communist on that occasion: "A Communist is a son-of-a-bitch who wants thirty cents an hour and you only want to pay him twenty-five cents."

Among other benefits, the strike brought to Salinas, during one of the more violent periods in the action, a contingent of San Francisco newspapermen, staunch Guildsmen all. I became well acquainted with them, now and then feeding them tidbits of news the *Index-Journal* would not print. They thought I should become a member of the Guild and were even so kind as to put me on the mailing list for the *Guild Reporter,* an overheated labor paper of about the same caliber as Harry Bridges' *Pacific Coast Longshoreman,* or whatever it was called then.

The Guild papers came to me at the office, and in my innocence I let them pile up behind my typewriter until the stack got too big, when they went into the wastebasket. From the casual glance I gave it occasionally, I thought it was a pretty sad excuse for a newspaper.

Not so the publisher, whose reaction was typical of the paranoia of the times. One day a friend of mine in the accounting department tipped me off that a check for two weeks' pay in lieu of notice had been prepared for me. He said he had heard on the grapevine that I was to be fired for suspected Guild activity!

I was startled, but not dismayed, at the utterly absurd action. I was still single, twenty-seven, and restless, the newspaper business was emerging from the Depression, and I had heard of other jobs. In fact, that night I did some telephoning and lined up a job, to take effect two weeks hence. (The job was on the *Mercury Herald,* where my old friend John Brokenshire was back in the saddle after an editorial department shakeup).

Sure enough, at the end of the week the managing editor called me into the front office, usually occupied by the publisher, who was out of town just then. He got around behind the big desk—where I couldn't reach him, I presume—and began a speech.

It had to do with my increasing skill and commensurate value as a reporter, surely approaching big-time status, but since the *Index-Journal* was having a hard time financially (a lie), it could not afford to pay me what I was worth, and therefore . . .

At this point I lost patience and told the poor, sweating individual to cut out the guff and give me the check, which I knew was reposing in the drawer in front of him. He did and I left.

On my way home for a vacation before starting my new job,

I stopped by to visit a friend, Llewellyn B. Peck, editor of the *Los Gatos Mail-News*. When he found out that I was "at liberty," he threw down his eyeshade and all but ran out the door.

"I've been trying to get a vacation for ten years," he shouted over his shoulder. "It's all yours!"

So I made another two weeks' pay and altogether had more cash in my jeans that I had ever before accumulated at one time. I even went out and made a down payment on a new Ford V-8 (total price, $850). I began to think that perhaps this Guild business was not so bad an idea after all.

The oddest part of the whole Salinas fiasco was, in my mind, the severance pay check itself, a completely unprecedented gesture and actually quite unnecessary one. It was the only severance pay I ever drew upon leaving any job, before or since. Severance pay was a key issue in all Guild negotiations of later years, as protection for the union's members whom the management might want to get rid of for any reason, but in 1936 it was unheard of in small-town newspapers.

I could only figure that the publisher was not taking any chances, not knowing just how hot a union agitator I might be, and not wanting to chance an invasion by Harry Bridges and his waterfront goons in support of their beleagured brother-in-arms.

The only thing I felt sure of was that the payment was not made out of the kindness of the publisher's heart, or at the insistence of his wife. I feel sure that my ribald remarks about the fudge—made at the Franciscan Hotel bar, where the staff repaired in a hurry after the presentation—got back to the publisher and his wife. We knew we had a stooge in our midst but usually did not care.

I guess I should not have said those unkind things about the fudge, at that. It really was not all that bad.

Oh, yes—perhaps I should add that I did thereafter become quite active in the Guild and helped to organize chapters in several California cities, including San Jose. I remained an active member until I left the newspaper game in 1942.

16

THE SALINAS LETTUCE WAR

In the previous chapter I mentioned the Salinas lettuce strike of 1936 in passing, but I think it is worth a chapter to itself. I still remember it as one of the most hectic periods in my newspaper career and as my first personal exposure to what I know now was one of the largest civil rights violations by constituted authority in California history.

Once, thirty years or so after the fact, I had the notion of doing a magazine piece about the strike (or the war, as it actually was). I went to Salinas to try to read the back files of the *Index-Journal* but found that all the old files had been reduced to microfilm (surely an invention of the Devil) and transferred to the county library.

At the library, however, I discovered that the two reels of microfilm covering the months in question were unaccountably missing. Perhaps if I had been more suspicious, I might have turned up a sinister plot, or if I had been more persistent, I might have found a local historian with bound files of the old paper. As it was, it did not seem worth the effort and I abandoned the project.

So, now I am entirely dependent upon my memory, which, though vivid in kaleidoscopic fashion, is spotty as to detail and uncertain as to sequence. Many things happened in only a couple of months, some of them more or less simultaneously, and perhaps the order does not matter now.

It all started, as I recall, with an effort by the agricultural workers, partly migrant and partly resident, to raise their base pay from twenty-five cents an hour to thirty cents an hour (which by John Steinbeck's definition automatically made them all Communists, as related in the previous chapter). When the loosely organized union, long before the days of Caesar Chavez, threatened to strike, the employers were ready. They locked the workers out—all of those who professed to be union members or were even suspected of union membership.

Soon after the lockout it became apparent that matters were going according to plan—the employers' plan—which was to bust the union wide open. Lettuce harvesting proceeded with nonunion labor working under armed guard. The trucks hauling lettuce to the packing sheds had men riding shotgun just as they did in the bad old days.

The packing also proceeded according to plan, in a compound obviously prepared in advance, behind a high wire fence patrolled by more armed guards. All the major packers cooperated in this public-spirited enterprise, which incidentally sent the price of lettuce sky high. A few of the smaller packers who tried to buck the Establishment soon found themselves cut off from ice, crates, and means of shipping their produce and were forced to give up.

Soon rumors of impending violence by the workers began to circulate. There was a report, never confirmed, that a dynamite cache in a quarry outside town had been robbed—a dastardly deed obviously laid at the door of the union. Who else would want the stuff, and what for?

An emergency meeting at the armory was called by the commander of the national guard, who in civilian life was a minor city official. He had his moment of glory. He said he had direct information that an army of longshoreman led by none other than Harry Bridges in person was marching on Salinas to assist their beleagured brethren. He produced a handful of little red flags he said he had found along the highway north of town, obviously placed there to indicate the line of march. He did not mention whether the invading army from San Francisco was advancing on foot, by truck, or on horseback over a distance of 110 miles.

He also produced a telegram he said was from the chief of police of Piedmont (a suburb of Oakland) of all places, warning the city of Salinas of the approaching multitude. I find it hard to believe now, even as I did then, that several hundred sober citizens would believe that sort of hysterical fiction, but they did. The commander even had a presumably loaded machine gun manned by a guardsman set up in the hall facing the door to repel any surprise attack. That gun made me mighty nervous, for I figured that if the guardsman were as far off his rocker as his boss there was no telling what might happen. (It was that same day, I believe, that all the citizens who had attended the meeting, and a few who had missed it, were issued white arm bands and ax handles with which to patrol the streets and guard them against invasion, or sabotage, or something.)

Of course, the San Francisco newspapermen were not at all taken in by the charade. Right after the rally they called the local office of the state highway department and learned that its engineers were pretty upset because some vandal had stolen all the little red survey markers they had just put out for a realignment job. Then the newsmen called the chief of police at Piedmont and learned that he had never heard of (1) a telegram to Salinas or (2) an invasion march. They tried to call Harry Bridges, but his office said he was in Hawaii and would not be back for a month. They also called all the other police chiefs around the Bay area and got a unanimous horse laugh for their pains.

Next, all the reporters drove out to Fly Hill, the shanty town where most of the lettuce workers lived, and had a hard time finding anyone to talk to. The wives of some of the men said they had all gone fishing and would not go near the city for fear of their lives.

And so it went, with very little except the official handouts appearing in the local paper.

The San Francisco papers were not so inhibited, nor was the *Monterey Peninsula Herald.* They reported the entire story, including the fiasco of the little red flags and the phony telegram. Soon, however, it became impossible to find any of those outside papers on the local newsstands, and the local populace went largely ignorant of the goings-on.

I heard that at one point a delegation from the growers and business community went to Monterey to protest the newspaper's coverage of the strike. The publisher met them in his office with a stenographer at his side. When the group demanded that she leave, the publisher informed them that their visit and everything they said and did there was news and would be reported in full.

The men ranted and raved but to no avail. The next day the *Peninsula Herald* carried a blow-by-blow account of the visit with verbatim transcription of all the threats and profanity. The group did not come back. Later I heard that one of the paper's principal advertisers bowed to pressure from the group and stopped its advertising, but that, too, was front page news in the *Peninsula Herald.* A boycott of the store by housewives took care of that situation.

In the meantime, the entire law enforcement authority of the city as well as that part of the county—including the police, the sheriff's office and the state highway patrol—somehow became centered in one office, a closely guarded hideout occupying the top floor of a downtown hotel. The office was headed by an unfrocked minister already famed for his strike-breaking activities. He was the self-proclaimed leader of an organization called the Citizen's League or some such misnomer. It was closely affiliated with a similar organization called the Associated Farmers. Both were so far out in right field they would have made Ronald Reagan look like a wild-eyed radical.

Before anyone outside that mysterious office knew what was happening, all news about the strike and any related activity in the city was being filtered through the office, whatever it purported to be. The result was an effective news blackout so far as the local press was concerned, but there were plenty of leaks to keep the men from the outside papers happily churning out copy, day after day. I can now confess, forty-odd years later, that I had a hand in springing some of those leaks.

One might wonder whether having all this red-hot news going on right under my nose when I was unable to get much of it printed did not drive me to drink. But I had a means, besides leaking the word to the other papers, of relieving my frustrations and at the same time augmenting my meager salary.

I sent nightly news stories, toned down somewhat from the more sensational San Francisco newspaper version, to the good old *San Jose Mercury Herald.* Warned in advance, the editors were careful not to identify the writer, and the stories appeared under an anonymous "Special to the Mercury Herald" by-line.

Not having a typewriter at the boarding house where I lived, (and not sure of the security there) I used to type my stories for the *Mercury Herald* at night at the *Index-Journal* office. Always I kept a letter addressed to "Dear Mom and Dad" close at hand to whip into the machine in case anyone happened to come in.

I never got caught, and nobody ever asked me if I knew who was writing those stories—if, indeed, anyone in Salinas ever saw them. However, some suspicion of my free-lance activities may well have contributed to my early departure from the *Index-Journal.* On the other hand, the same stories probably helped me to get a job at the *Mercury Herald* soon after I left Salinas. I feel quite certain that all my extracurricular activities during that period did not go unnoticed, especially the time I informed one of the San Francisco newspapermen that a posse was on his trail with some discourtesy in mind, and then helped to spirit him out of town on a chartered plane minutes ahead of the posse.

Sometime well along in the war, we reporters became aware of the presence in town of a couple of dozen burly men in overcoats and hard hats. They were, we discovered, imported from Los Angeles. Nowadays they would be called enforcers. What they were enforcing, it seems, was a 9 P.M. curfew imposed by the mayor under some mythical authority. Actually, the curfew was rather silly, since the town usually rolled up the sidewalks at dark and, in those days, no sane union member would have ventured onto the streets after working hours.

I found out about the enforcers personally one night when I was walking home after working late at the paper, paying no heed to the curfew which was pretty much of a joke around town anyhow. An open automobile screeched to a stop by the curb and I found myself seized in a double hammer lock by two of these thugs. Much too scared to stand on my rights, I told them I was a local reporter and produced a press pass to prove it.

They let me go with a warning to stay off the streets at night. They said it was not safe. I did not dispute the matter, but wrote a brief account for the paper. It did not get printed. In retrospect, it seems to me that quite a few things I wrote during that period did not get printed, at least not in the *Index-Journal*. Perhaps there was not enough room.

The next major event in the strike was a series of dynamite blasts (presumably from that missing cache). Oddly enough, none of the blasts ever did much damage. One wrecked an old truck in a vacant lot, abandoned there for months. Another blast tore up the thistles near the packing shed compound but only made a big noise. For several nights running, I rolled out of bed to cover the latest explosion, but after the first two or three nobody seemed much interested. Of course, the blasts were officially blamed on the Communists, whoever they were.

Late in the war, with no warning, the convoys of lettuce trucks coming in from the field suddenly started rolling right down the main street of town, instead of following a bypass route they usually took. By then the price of lettuce had gone out of sight, from something like five cents a head to five times that amount. It was almost nonobtainable in the local stores, since every usable head was being express shipped to the eastern market. I saw otherwise dignified matrons run out into the street to pick up heads of lettuce that fell off the trucks.

One day the trucks and their armed escort were confronted by a wall of resistance, a mass of several hundred lettuce workers who jammed the street in the heart of the city. I never did learn how and why they were there—I was told they had been lured into the city under some pretext of negotiations and then were herded into the center of town by state police. But by then I had come not to trust any statements by anybody on either side, for the truth was by all odds the biggest loser in the war.

In any case, it turned out to be a highly tense moment when the shotgun guard of the growers and packers came face to face with the more militant of the workers, some of whom were armed with baseball bats and a few were brandishing revolvers. It was a very dangerous situation, of the sort where anything could have happened.

Just at the crucial moment, however, a police captain, whose name eludes me, walked out into the middle of the intersection, between the hostile factions, and held up his arms for silence. Perhaps it was the shock effect that did the job, but whatever it was, it worked.

Turning to the farmers, the police captain ordered them to back up their trucks and take them down the back street where they belonged. Then he told the workers to go home and stay there before somebody got hurt. They all obeyed him with alacrity, all doubtless happy to have a face-saving way out of that parlous predicament. It was an exhibition of cool nerve, for if the shooting had started, he would have been right in the middle.

What he did certainly was not in the script, and it obviously thwarted whatever scheme had been behind the confrontation. No doubt he was censored for his impromptu act, but I don't think that gave him much concern. He was still on the job after the lettuce war was all over.

My lifelong regret is that I missed the action with my camera, although I was perfectly set up for it. By chance, I was the only news photographer in the right place at the right time, on top of a two-story building overlooking the scene, with my back to the sun. All the other reporters and cameramen had been caught on the wrong side of the street, blocked by the mob.

At the high point of the action, just as the police captain walked into the scene, I tripped the shutter on the big 4 x 5 Graflex and then yanked on the paper tab of the film pack to pull the next exposure into place. In my excitement, I yanked too hard and jerked the entire film pack out of its box. It fell streaming into the street amid the jeers of the crowd, some of whom had been throwing rocks at me earlier. *Index-Journal* reporters were not highly regarded by the workers just then. Quickly I reached for my backup camera, a small folding Kodak of my own, and shot up the rest of the roll of film that was in it. Then I rushed the film to the local commercial photographer for immediate processing, since the newspaper had no darkroom.

Later that afternoon I learned to my horror that someone new in the camera shop had developed the film, which was fast panchromatic, under a safelight and it was all fogged beyond recovery. I guess every news photographer has at least one such experience in his lifetime, to brood about in his declining years.

Perhaps that courageous action by the police captain served to point up the utter absurdity of the whole business. If it was not that episode, then it was some other one I have forgotten, that led to the breaking up of that infamous growers' cabal, which by then was under furious attack by the American Civil Liberties Union. The townspeople, especially the business community, had had enough, for the ordinary business affairs of the town were severely disrupted throughout the affair.

Somehow the district attorney persuaded the local superior judge to issue a restraining order which, in effect, told the leader of the strike-breaking organization to get out of town. He did, the various law enforcement agencies resumed their normal activities, and things got back to normal—minus the union. It was a long time before the union became effective as a bargaining agent for the workers, but by then I was back on the *Mercury Herald* helping to organize a union of our own.

17

"THIS OLD SCOW"

MY FIRST JOB when I returned to the *San Jose Mercury Herald* in 1937 was in the role of county editor, sometimes called state editor. I had charge of news from all the outlying towns in the newspaper's circulation area. Ordinarily, I had to fight for space, but for the Sunday edition I had two full pages, face to face, with no advertising to clutter it up anywhere.

With an eye to design—a conceit of all makeup editors—I took pride in the physical appearance of my pages. For this particular occasion, I balanced the layouts of the opposing pages with two 2-column photos looking at each other across the fold. They were exactly the same size—something I learned then and there never to do again. It was just the loophole Murphy had been waiting for. Remember Murphy? I had forgotten about him too.

One of the two photos was a portrait of the retiring postmistress of one of the outlying towns. Both she and the town must remained unidentified for a reason that shortly will become obvious. The opposite photo was of an ancient barge that had just been resurrected from the mud at Alviso, a onetime seaport on lower

San Francisco Bay, where it had sunk in a sensational wreck seventy-five years before. Part of its bow and a gaping hawsehole leered at the reader with an eerie and grotesque resemblance to a human face.

By now you have no doubt figured out what Murphy did. He switched the captions. Under the portrait of the retiring postmistress the caption read: "This old scow was dredged up from the mud at Alviso." Naturally, the picture of the barge said it was the postmistress.

Now I can only explain what happened next by saying that Murphy was sleepy, as it was getting on to midnight. Or perhaps by that time I had developed some sort of subconscious sixth sense for looming disaster, after seven years on newspapers.

I do know that I had nothing consciously gnawing at the back of my mind when I went down to the pressroom late that night. It was the first and only time I ever watched that newspaper come off the press in all the eight years I worked there.

The head pressman handed me one of the first copies, all fresh and smelling strongly of that beguiling perfume called printer's ink. Automatically, I turned to my two pages. For a long moment I stared at the pages and their transposed captions, and then (again for the first and only time in my newspaper life) I yelled, "Stop the press!"

The head pressman, thinking I was making a bad joke, strolled over to where I was standing and asked what was going on. Mutely, I pointed to the pictures. He was an old hand and needed no urging. He ran to the control board and yanked the main switch. The press ground to a halt.

Then he and I and the entire press gang rounded up and counted every last copy and ceremoniously burned them in a trash barrel in the alley outside. I even chased a cop down the street a block to retrieve a early copy he had picked up. We did not keep a single copy for a souvenir. Meanwhile, the composing room, alerted by the sudden stopping of the press, had got the message and was making over the two pages. They went back on the press after close inspection at about six levels.

All of us, I am certain, had it in mind that the newspaper had just made an out-of-court settlement over a libel suit in a much less harmful error. No jury could have been persuaded that *my* error was an accident, under the circumstances, and the defense never could have brought Murphy's Law into the case.

Perhaps I should have mentioned that the reason I had just been given the job of county editor was because the previous occupant of the position was the man who had made the previous error that brought on the libel suit. Even if the newspaper had survived the inevitable second suit financially, my personal fate would have been certain.

18

JOHN BROKENSHIRE'S BIGGEST FISH

"The gods do not subtract from the allotted span of men's lives the time spent in fishing"

The Assyrians.

ONE EPISODE on the brighter side of a sometimes dismal newspaper job late in the Great Depression keeps coming back to mind. It involved a good friend and occasional fishing companion, John R. Brokenshire, on the occasion of a fishing trip in 1937. This was not long before John quit the city editorship of the old *San Jose Mercury Herald* to go into adult education.

The time was spring in the Lassen country of northern California, where a bunch of us boys were whooping it up deep in the wilderness. There we had been hauled in a truck over some terrible roads by John's brother, Wesley, who was then district ranger for the U.S. Forest Service.

I have forgotten who all was in the party other than the two Brokenshires; John's teenage son Jack, Dwight Bentel, head of the

San Jose State College journalism department; Leslie Stapp, a Los Gatos real estate man, and myself.

It was a deluxe expedition. We had tents, big thick mattresses, cots, and an expert camp cook in the person of Wes Brokenshire. We caught a great many trout, none of them over six inches long, which Wes served up piping hot after deep-frying them in bacon fat over a campfire. We ate them by the dozen, bones and all. Nothing was ever more delicious.

One afternoon I strolled back into camp with my usual bag of barely legal minnows to find the rest of our party already assembled for happy hour around the campfire. It was immediately apparent that something was afoot. The atmosphere of expectancy was all but palpable. Knowing these men quite well, I stopped short for a careful look around. Any sort of practical joke was possible, even probable, with the last man in as the victim.

The only alien note I could detect was a suspiciously conspicuous wet gunny sack hanging from a tree limb. I went over to take a cautious peek, as obviously I was supposed to. I took one look and sat down flat in amazement. The sack covered the largest trout I had ever seen in the wild.

To be exact, I should say it was the *longest* trout I had ever seen in the wild, or anywhere else, measuring slightly more than twenty-six inches from stem to stern—but more about the vital statistics later. With very little persuasion, John agreed to tell the tale, as he did at least fifty-nine times in the ensuing days and weeks.

"I was sitting on this big boulder overlooking a deep pool, see, half dozing in the sun while enjoying a pipe, when I saw a large drifting shadow in the water right below me. I knew it had to be a fish, or a baby alligator," he began.

Carefully John retrieved his line and tied on a large hook with a gob of angleworms or salmon eggs or something tasty, and just as carefully lowered the lure into the water right in front of the big shadow. The result was instant chaos. It would have made a great movie.

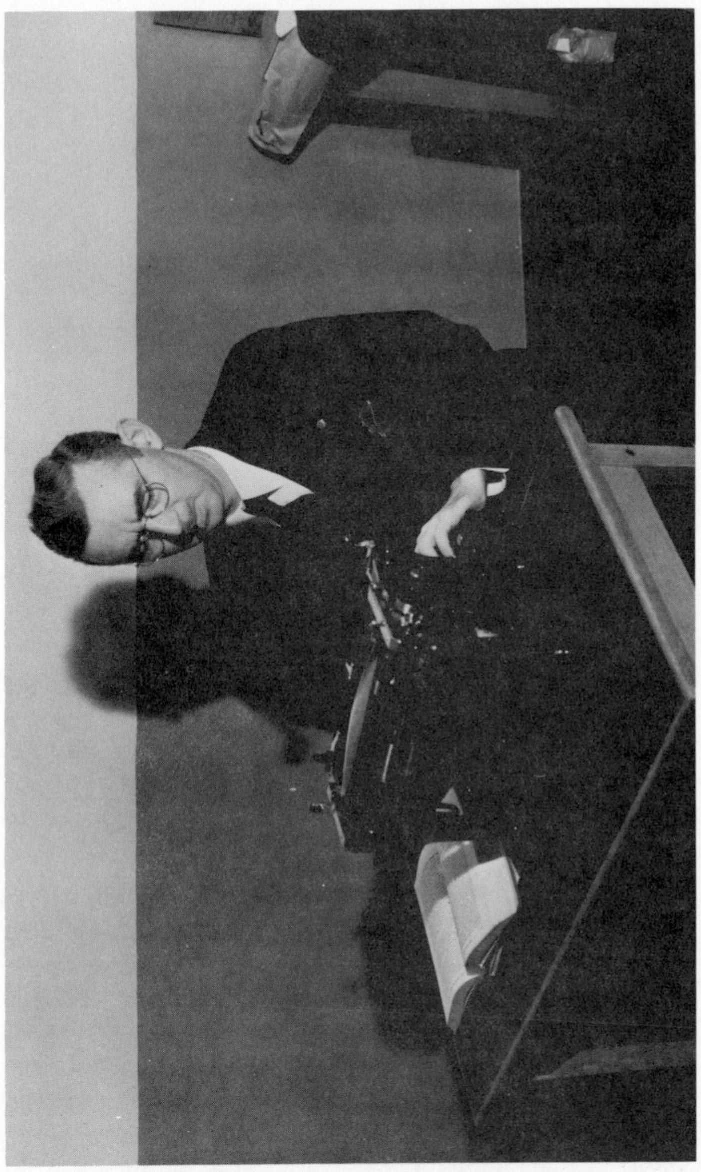

John Brokenshire at work. (DWIGHT BENTEL)

We, of course, had only John's version of all that went on. It was not that we doubted his veracity, but he was a fisherman. He claimed that he waltzed around on top of the rock for half an hour, trying to haul in his prize, and finally in sheer desperation jumped into the pool to grapple with the fish. We opined (out loud) that he simply fell in, probably right off the bat.

In any case, it was certain that John did find himself up to his mustache in the pool along with his pipe, his glasses, his rod and all his gear. The fish was there too, still firmly attached to the lure, which it had managed to swallow entirely. Somehow, John struggled ashore, towing the fish. I think he must have run all the way back to camp with the monster, not even stopping to unhook it.

Now I must relate that the fish was not much larger around than a Lassie League baseball bat. Instead of weighing the fifteen to eighteen pounds its length ordinarily would call for, it scaled out (if you will pardon the expression) at less than four pounds. In fact, it was mostly head and backbone.

All of us except John argued that it was a spent steelhead that somehow had missed out on its return trip to the sea after spawning upstream the previous winter, and had become trapped in the big pool when the stream level went down. That happens sometimes—steelhead, the seagoing phase of the rainbow trout, are capable of making many round trips between the ocean and their freshwater spawning grounds, unlike their cousins, the salmon, who make the upstream journey only once and then die.

We insisted that taking steelhead out of season was illegal, and that John should have put the poor thing back alive. Since he had not done so, we said his brother should arrest him on behalf of the state game warden and confiscate the fish for charity. Wes agreed, but said he had left his handcuffs at home, and anyhow he did not know of any local charity desperate enough to accept the gift.

Highly indignant, John insisted that the trout was a legitimate member of the rainbow species complete with colors, etc., etc. He argued that it could not have been a spent steelhead since they do not feed until they reach salt water after spawning, hence his prize would not have accepted the lure, etc., etc. He was deaf to the counterargument that steelhead have been known to strike at a lure out of anger or frustration or whatever.

In the end, of course, we all had to stop laughing and pay our respects to the fish and take the ritualistic pictures of John holding it up (with two hands). Then we packed up and went home, and forgot about the fish. At least, John thought we had forgotten about it.

Back at the *Mercury Herald,* however, it had not been forgotten, even after John tired of telling about it and showing off the photos. We even suggested that we should do a story about it, but we vetoed the idea on the grounds that editors never make news, only report it.

Surrepticiously and with some help from John's wife, June, the staff at the paper concocted a long and mostly accurate story about the trip and its sensational conclusion. The report started out a month before the trip when John, according to June, got that annual dreamy look and started to sort out his fishing gear. When he began to practice fly casting in the garden at the expense of the petunias, June looked anxiously at the calendar, hoping May 1 would arrive before the flowers were all gone. She knew that the sooner he went fishing, the better for all.

We recounted the story of the capture, and topped it all off with a two-column photo of John and the fish, reading left to right. Nearly everyone on the news staff had a hand in the production and the printing department men went along with the gag with glee. It was a great project.

When all was ready, we waited for John to go home one Saturday night after the Sunday morning paper had been put to bed. Then we quickly substituted our story for one on the first page of the second section, where we had dummied in some innocuous feature of the same size. Now I do not remember whether we let the fish story run through the entire edition, or merely ran off a few dozen copies and then returned to the original feature. In any case, we made sure one of the fishing versions found its way to Brokenshire's front porch before morning.

John came in the next afternoon with fire in his eye, but he often had fire in his eye so that was not unusual. He had only one good eye and it was electric blue, capable of shooting sparks on occasion. He marched down to the copy desk and glared at each of us gathered there to face the music. "You guys are all fired," he barked, and went back to his desk.

Naturally, nobody was alarmed at his summary dismissal nor did anyone holler for the shop steward (not that we had one—the Guild was strictly underground in those days). We all took his remark in the spirit in which it was offered—as sincere praise for our combined journalistic enterprise. Coming from Brokenshire, who was by all odds the finest newspaperman I ever knew, that was an accolade to be treasured, as it still is in my mind after half a century.

John died in 1979 at the age of eighty-three, but not before he and Dwight Bentel and I were able to get together for some good laughs over the episode of the big fish and other incidents of our many trips together into the wild of California (when there were still some wilds to venture into). I have little doubt that John is still fishing some Elysian stream, trying to top that twenty-six-incher and waiting for us with fire in his eye to argue over its validity.

This episode came back to me again even more recently, when on a trip through northern California my wife and I noticed a road sign on State Highway 36 in Lassen County, pointing down a side road to Mill Creek. Since we wanted to have a picnic lunch, we took the turnoff and shortly found ourselves at a forest service roadside rest stop with a sign that said:

BROKENSHIRE PICNIC AREA
—1959—

It had been named for John's brother Wesley, in honor of his many years as the district forest supervisor. It was, by the map, not many miles from the scene of John's big fish, but without a guide I never could have hoped to find the exact spot.

19

THE CRAZY FOREST

YOU WILL NOT FIND IT on any map or in any historical reference work, simply because it existed for only a short time in a remote part of the Santa Cruz mountain range and then vanished forever.

The Crazy Forest, as it was known locally, came into being abruptly one morning three quarters of a century ago, and then disappeared thirty-odd years later, as an obscure little patch of virgin redwoods covering perhaps fifty acres.

The great trees towered majestically on either side of the narrow east work of Soquel creek, near the crest of the watershed in the Loma Prieta country, not far from Buzzard Lagoon. The grove was called the Crazy Forest because it contained the craziest-looking bunch of redwood trees ever seen by mortal man. Many of them grew not straight up to the sky like proper redwoods but at all angles including the horizontal.

This strange state of affairs happened all at once on the morning of April 18, 1906, when the great San Francisco earthquake

Crazy Forest, 1937 (DWIGHT BENTEL)

came rattling and banging along the San Andreas fault. The fault, or one of its branches, runs right up Soquel Creek at this place.

Giant redwoods were growing on the steep banks of the creek, which in that section was a deeply carved V-shaped gulch following the curious zig-zag coarse of an earthquake rift. The trees were still there because of the steep terrain and remote location. Heavy rains had preceded the earthquake and softened the banks, loosening the precarious anchorage of the big trees.

When the earthquake struck, hundreds of the trees toppled like 200-foot jackstraws. Many of them, falling toward the creek from both sides, entangled their tops and upper branches and could fall no farther. They remained standing at weird angles, forming an awesome, cathedral-like ceiling far above the creek.

Others fell flat, bringing down wide swaths of other trees, but leaving their roots embedded in the soft banks, forming broad living bridges over the gulch. The few trees left standing in their natural state provided the only vertical reference for the viewer to determine which way was up.

And that's the way the grove had remained through three decades, a generation by human standards but no more than an eye-blink for a sequoia. Soon the uppermost branches of the prostrate but living trees grew into new trees. The inclined trees with interlocking tops grew new tops, and all together they formed an immense green canopy over an incredible jumble of limbs and logs.

When I first visited the grove, in the spring of 1937, it was just barely possible to follow the creek on foot by scrambling over and among the downed trees, at times crossing the creek on horizontal trunks thirty or forty feet above the water. Even the trees that had died in the maelstrom were still sound of trunk, since redwood never rots. The bark was gone, as were the leaves and twigs and smaller branches, but the huge boles were intact, as they might have remained for centuries but for man's blind greed.

The green canopy seemed to have produced a kind of microclimate, a greenhouse effect that encouraged the growth of native

Crazy Forest, 1937 (DWIGHT BENTEL)

ferns to an amazing degree. Woodwardia and redwood ferns grew higher than my head, as if they were in a tropical jungle or a botanical garden under glass.

Brilliant scarlet and yellow monkey flowers crowded the edges of the little stream, competing with penstemons, oxalis and wood violets for attention. Mosses, lichens and tiny plants of many varieties covered the earth and most of the rocks and logs.

At the time I was there, ladybugs were migrating, swarming over rocks, logs and bushes in countless millions, making passage almost impossible. It was as if hundreds of gallons of bright red-orange paint had been spilled over the mass of fallen timber. I have seen ladybug swarms elsewhere since then but never in such vast legions as they were that day in the Crazy Forest.

The air was warm and humid under the canopy, although outside it was a mild spring day. From the rank growth I had the idea this was a more or less constant state that winter seldom penetrated. The deeply shaded water was cool enough for trout and I saw many darting about, but fishing in that tangle would have been fruitless had I been so inclined.

It was the kind of place where one could sit by the hour, soaking up the ambience of peace and lush natural beauty, but it was a long way out of there and no place to be caught after dark, so I left, reluctantly. I had been so caught up in the magic of the little sylvan paradise that I had quite forgotten for the moment why I was there in the first place, that here was in fact a unique, living relic of the 1906 earthquake, probably the most outstanding of all natural records of the event.

I spent some time trying to record the incredible scene on black-and-white film. One trouble was that the growth everywhere was so dense it was impossible to find any clear vantage point among the trees; from above it all looked like nothing more than a solid mass of greenery. I needed pictures badly for my purpose, which was to sell a freelance article—the first I had ever attempted—to a San Francisco newspaper to run on the anniversary of the earthquake, which was April 18. My negatives were dated 4/4/37, which did not allow much time for second guessing.

I sent the article about the Crazy Forest, with a set of prints, to the *San Francisco Chronicle.* When I heard nothing from it after several days, I went off for a weekend visit in the Sierra foothills. There the *Chronicle* Sunday editor tracked me down by phone. He wanted more and better photos, right now.

Of course, I was much too far away to do him any good (and I knew I could not improve on the photos I had made), so I referred him to the man who had told me about the place—the Santa Cruz County farm agent. I warned the editor that it was a rugged trip, but I guess he did not believe me, for he sent in a staff photographer anyhow.

Later the farm agent told me about that expedition. It seems the road had been washed out in a cloudburst a few days after I had been in there, and it had been necessary to trek overland a couple of miles to reach the canyon. They did not make it all the way.

Encumbered by a heavy camera case (news photographers mostly carried 4 x 5 Speed Graphics in those days) and a tripod, plus a city-style business suit with collar and tie, not to mention low-cut shoes, the chain-smoking and overweight city dude could not hack it. He folded up well short of the objective, and the farm agent almost had to carry him out.

So, the *Chronicle* had to satisfy itself with my photos, but it took revenge by using only one picture about postage-stamp size and by chopping the article down to half a column. Still, a check for even ten dollars was welcome in those days, although I had been counting on getting at least twice that amount.

After that I helped the Sierra Club and some other conservation groups in a last-ditch effort to try to save the grove for a public park of some sort, but like so many other efforts of its kind at the time, it was a case of too little, too late. Nobody had money to spare for a public preserve in the back of beyond. Ironically, the grove might well have been included in the Forest of Nisene Marks, which it adjoined, when that 9000-acre tract became a state park in the 1960s.

A couple of years later I drove over Highland Way to see if the Crazy Forest had survived. I was sorry I did so, for the forest was gone, its site an utter disaster. Bulldozers were yanking logs out of the gulch, now a dusty hellhole. Both banks of the erstwhile trout stream had been reduced to naked red earth over a shambles of broken limbs, shattered tree trunks, and all the nightmare debris of a ruthless logging operation of the period.

Perhaps worst of all was the gut-level realization that this was forever, that these scars could never be entirely healed even in a region of rapid forest regeneration. Not only were the trees gone, and the flowers and ferns and even the fish, but most of the topsoil as well, washed down into the creek bottom to form a muddy slough in a soup of mangled vegetation.

Earthquakes inevitably will rattle the rocks and split the hillsides along the San Andreas fault from time to time in the future as they have for the past hundred million years, but none can ever again create a Crazy Forest. Like lost, lovely Glen Canyon on the Colorado, the Crazy Forest was not only unique but irreplaceable.

20

PHOTOGRAPHERS ARE FUNNY PEOPLE

THE CRAZY FOREST episode was only one of many in which news photographers played a major role, both in my own experience and in the large stock of legends which have grown up around that odd fraternity.

Although I have owned a camera of one kind or another for more than sixty years and have made innumerable photos for newspapers and magazines, I have never worked full time at the trade and thus do not consider myself a member of the Esoteric Order of Newspaper Photographers. However, as a reporter, feature writer and editor and as a free-lance journalist, I have worked closely with many top-notch photographers and treasure many recollections that to me reflect the spirit of the times, especially times gone by.

News photos were, until the advent of TV, the only means of giving the public on-the-spot views of events in the news while it was still news, and they played a vital part in daily newspaper coverage. Big city newspapers in the late 1930s produced fine-screen sepia-toned picture supplements by the process called rotogravure, which at times turned out really excellent reproductions.

But the demands of editors, especially those on highly competitive metropolitan papers, often approached the absurd. A famous case in point developed during the 1914–17 volcanic eruptions at Mt. Lassen. The eruptions had been in the news for some time, but now lava was flowing down the mountain and promised some sensational pictures. The editors doubtless had visions of villages being innundated, although there were no villages anywhere near the lava.

Of course, it was midwinter and snowing by then, and the roads were closed by weather and by the danger of the lava flows. The closest any of the several metropolitan newspaper photographers and reporters who had been sent to cover the story could get to the scene was a roadside tavern at Mineral, nearly twenty miles away. Nevertheless the photographers were constantly besieged by their editors with telegrams demanding pictures—any kind of pictures, if not of the actual lava flow, then some of the volcano's mushroom cloud of smoke and ashes.

Since they had no means of aerial transportation, there was nothing the photographers could do but wait, filling in the time with a marathon poker game and sundry refreshments.

At one point, a photographer whose name I have forgotten staggered out the back door of the tavern in response to an urgent call. The outhouse was situated just past the stable yard. In the yard was an enormous heap of manure, steaming in the frigid night air.

Now, the photographer had taken on a considerable load of booze, but not so much so his instincts were dulled. His primary mission completed, he slipped back into the tavern, gathered up his equipment while nobody was looking, and returned to the yard. There he made several time exposures of the manure pile, first augmenting the effect by using a long stick to make a crater in the top of the heap. He counted on the falling snow to render the subject suitably fuzzy.

His photos went out by stage that afternoon and in due course appeared on the front page of his San Francisco newspaper. The photographer had enclosed a note giving instructions on processing the film, but had carefully refrained from stating that they were pictures of the volcano. He could not help it if the editor took that for granted and so captioned the picture.

After sober reflection, the photographer realized that his name would be mud with his fellows when the competition saw his picture, so he packed up and left the next morning, assuming that his editor would agree that he had completed his assignment.

Naturally, there was hell to pay when the picture appeared, resulting in a torrent of telegrams to the other photographers at Mineral. In vain they protested that the picture had to be a fake. The culprit, back home, sat tight and refused to divulge how he had obtained the photo, hinting that he had bribed some official to let him past the roadblock and had to protect his benefactor.

He never did tell anybody but a few close friends how he made that picture and the story did not come out until after his death twenty-odd years later when a Bay area columnist did a "now-it-can-be-told" piece about the escapade.

At the other end of the scale in news photography was an incident I will always remember. We had a young trainee photographer on the *Mercury Herald* staff, just out of school and full of zeal. I will call him Bill because that was not his name.

I had assigned him to cover a speech being delivered by Robert Gordon Sproul, president of the University of California, at the San Jose State College graduation exercises. He was told to try to get a good action shot with the speaker waving his arms or something suitable.

I did not actually see the execution of the assignment, but I heard about it in detail from several sources. Bill marched out on the stage where the speaker was in full cry, plunked his heavy camera case down on the floor with a crash, then assembled his Speed Graphic and flashgun with considerable clatter and capped the performance by firing off the flash practically in the speaker's face.

Bill had been told to get more than one shot, so he did it again. By that time the audience was in stitches and the speaker was having a terrible time maintaining his usually formidable dignity. Bill folded up his equipment, stuffed it in the case and tromped off the stage. He had a couple of pretty good shots, if you overlooked a rather frozen look on Dr. Sproul's face.

Then there was the time that Loris Gardner, the *Mercury Herald's* chief photographer—and one of the best in the business—had to go out with the society editor on a dreary assignment. It was to make a picture of the board of directors of a local hospital auxiliary, a group of women well past their prime and about as photogenic as a sack of potatoes.

The board was meeting in the society editor's home, a mid-Victorian pile in the older residential district, a place of high ceilings and massive dark woodwork. Loris was baffled, as he could see no way to make a usable photo under the circumstances. Stalling for time, he asked the young society editor if they could step into the next room to confer for a moment and opened the first door he came to. It led into the bathroom.

Loris sat on the edge of the tub and the society editor sat on the throne while they conferred. When they arose, the society editor automatically pulled the chain, providing a noisy and startling accompaniment to their exit. Loris said that if he could have sneaked a shot of the faces of the board of directors, it would have made the front page of *Life* Magazine, if it did not shatter the lens.

Then there was Barney Murphy, a legend in his time, a San Francisco newspaper photographer famous for his utter disregard for rank. He believed firmly that all men (and women) put on their pants one leg at a time and treated everyone accordingly. I have doubt that he snapped a shot of St. Peter as he entered the Pearly Gates, if he ever made it there.

Murphy obviously never heard of lese majeste. When the king

and queen of Siam (now Thailand) visited the United States, Barney was in the front row in the Palace Hotel ballroom where the royal entourage had consented to line up for a photograph. The queen stood at one end of the line and the king at the other. The king, a shy and modest little man, was a bit off to the side.

At this point Barney, from his vantage point down front, cried out, "Hey, king! If you want to get in this picture, move over!" The king did.

On another occasion the queen of Greece (I think it was) was being entertained at an improptu rodeo at a large cattle ranch in San Benito County. She was standing by the enclosure trying to see between the rails. Barney was on top of the fence trying to get a picture of her with a suitable background.

He patted the top of the nearest foot-square post and said, "Park it up here, sister." She did, and Barney got his picture.

John Brokenshire, my old city editor, who first hired me on the *Mercury Herald,* had a vividly descriptive name for a really top-grade news photo, the kind that is given a lot of front-page space, like the one of the Mt. Lassen eruption. He called such pictures "Jesus Christ photos" on the grounds that they were calculated to make the reader to exclaim, "Jesus Christ, look at this!"

I can recall having made just one such photo, largely by chance. I was on my way into the office one afternoon when I saw a large crowd and some flashing red lights on a side street. It turned out to be a workman buried up to his neck in a ditch. Our young photographer, Bill, was there all right, but he was down in the ditch. I thought that if the man were dead or out of sight, the picture would be unusable.

I had a camera but no flash, and no way to get through the solid ranks of onlookers without a bulldozer. Anyhow, an overhead shot seemed to be indicated. Up on the boom of the ditchdigging machine hanging over the ditch were several spectators, one of whom I knew. I called to him and made motions to show that I wanted to get up there to shoot a picture. He spoke to the others on the boom and they moved over so I could crawl up to the top. From that precarious perch, with my friend hanging onto my legs, I made several exposures of the scene straight down below.

The result was sensational. All the onlookers were staring down into the ditch, transfixed by the drama unfolding below, where men were frantically digging. They all were frozen in their positions as if they knew I was trying to make a picture with a slow exposure and no flash. The fact that the deep gloom of the ditch revealed nothing of what was happening in it only added to the suspense. The photo ran two columns wide the length of the front page.

For once, I did not forget to pull the dark slide, did not forget to set the shutter correctly, and did *not* pull the film pack all the way out of the camera in my excitement.

High school science teachers of half a century or so ago used to have their students make pinhole cameras out of shoe boxes as an experiment to demonstrate principles of photography. Perhaps they still do, although they are more likely to use a Polaroid for faster results. In my case, the lesson went home, and resulted many years later in an amusing journalistic tour de force.

For the benefit of any reader who was denied the privilege of trying this primitive but effective bit of physics, a pinhole punched in the end of a light-tight box will serve as a lens for a very old kind of camera. If a sheet of film or sensitized paper is inserted inside the opposite end of the box, and the apparatus then aimed at a suitable stationary subject, a photographic image will result, in time. Lots of time. Like a couple of hours in bright light if photographic paper is used. The image will be soft and grainy, but everything from about an inch in front of the box to infinity will be in focus, more or less.

Once long ago I put together a large-scale pinhole camera, measuring 16 by 18 inches by 24 inches long, with a 0.040 inch aperature drilled in a thin sheet of metal for the pinhole lens. I built it to accommodate an 11-by-14-inch glass plate holder of the type once used by studio photographers. I had picked up the plate holder and 10 badly outdated 11-by-14-inch Tri-X glass-plate negatives at a bargain counter somewhere, and felt I had to do something with them.

I soon used up the glass-plate negatives on various still lifes with varying degrees of success and then lost interest. Years later, I dusted off the big box for a caper cooked up in cahoots with a photographer friend, Alexander Lowry of Santa Cruz (who also was a refugee from the San Jose newspaper scene).

What we had in mind was a tongue-in-the-cheek pseudo-technical article involving the pinhole for a popular photography magazine. While camping in Yosemite one spring, we carted the pinhole camera, its plate holder loaded with outdated sheet color film, up to Washburn Point on the Glacier Point road, overlooking the Valley and the falls beyond. It was a lovely scene and would have made a fine picture, as it has countless times for other Ansel Adams types.

We set the box up on two tripods, aimed it in the general direction of the falls, draped a black cloth over the back and took turns photographing each other ostensibly operating the pinhole. We each had on a tee shirt with the words OFFICIAL PHOTOGRAPHER emblazoned across the back.

In the midst of this activity, I became aware that we had an interested spectator. He looked like a character straight out of a George Price cartoon, complete with pith helmet, pot belly, and cameras and light meters slung around his neck. When I looked up at him, he ventured closer, and in a confidential whisper (so as not to disturb the artist at work) asked me what kind of camera we were using. I told him it was a pinhole camera.

He seemed to know what that was and stood back, pondering the information. Then he asked, "What are the advantages of a pinhole camera?"

That stumped me, so I tapped Al on the shoulder. He emerged from under the black cloth to see what I wanted.

"This gentleman wants to know the advantages of the pinhole camera," I told him.

Al in turn pondered the subject, stroking his chin with due solemnity. Then he gave his expert opinion.

"There are no advantages," he pronounced, and ducked back under the black cloth. The coward—I could see his shoulders shaking.

Our visitor stared at us with his mouth open for a long moment, then he turned and hastened away, doubtless to report to his wife waiting in their Lincoln that he had run into a nest of kooks.

Perhaps he was right, at that. We got no pictures with the pinhole monster then or later. When we developed the negatives we found they were all too badly fogged to be of any value. Over the years, it seems, the wooden plate holder had dried out and had sprung several large light leaks in the corners.

For the curious, the camera had an equivalent focal length (lens to film distance) of 24 inches and the aperature at 0.040 inch was the equivalent of an f-stop of 640 or thereabouts. Under ideal conditions it produced some nice images of the spit-on-the-lens school.

21

YOU CAN'T GET A PACK TRIP LIKE THIS ANYMORE

WHEN I WASN'T SCOURING the countryside for news, I was dreaming of a trip to the high country. I made it in 1937; in 1969 I wrote this piece about it for the *New York Times*:

I would like some day to try one of those deluxe two-week high-country pack trips I read about in the travel literature. According to the advertisements, all one has to do is to lounge around on a foam-padded cot while the wranglers turn chef to prepare gourmet meals for appetites whetted to a razor edge by the day's riding through lush alpine meadows on well-trained, grain-fed horses that could find their way in a fog.

For breakfast, the chefs will prepare those easily caught, firm-fleshed mountain trout taken on your fly rod that morning, with a side order of eggs Benedict and Canadian bacon, all washed down with aromatic campfire coffee served in bone china on a white tablecloth—well, maybe a red-checkered one.

When I do this I am going to keep a careful diary for point-to-point comparison with my recollections of the first trip I ever ventured on—one that I can recall only too well even after forty years.

Oddly enough, I can still remember the few bright spots much better than the many drab ones: long lazy days spent jogging along granite-topped ridges far above chains of twinkly sapphire lakes; evening campfires, redolent of cedar, in parklike glades beside nameless streams; grassy meadows filled with wildflowers as high as our stirrups; marmots whistling at us from the rocks; jays and squirrels scolding from the spruce and fir trees; foamy white waterfalls tumbling over granite cliffs; the zestful tang of high-mountain air drenched with sun-distilled pine scent; the astonishing size and brightness of stars hanging low over a wilderness a hundred miles from a street light.

With only a little more effort but less pleasure I can reconstruct the other side of the scene, starting with the five members of our little company and our strange assortment of livestock.

Three of us were in our twenties—two newspapermen and a dairy farmer. The fourth was a middle-aged real estate salesman who had rheumatism he had not mentioned. The fifth was a seventeen-year-old farm hand-cum-horse wrangler named Henry, the only member of the party who knew what he was doing most of the time.

I do not recall just how such a group came to be assembled. I do recall that our mounts consisted of one ancient but able cow pony with a badly healed wire cut on one leg that gave him an interesting limp; one young Belgian draft mare of vast proportions that had never been ridden but did not seem to mind the experience in the least; one half-broken young sorrel that never wanted to be saddled again (only Henry could even get near her); another horse whose features I do not remember; a pack mule of great wisdom and experience in shucking off pack saddles; and a venerable burro of quite unpredictable behavior and the agility of a mountain goat.

Since the time was still during the Great Depression, at least for all of us, the rest of our equipment was on a par with our livestock—barely minimal for the job, looking like the leftovers from a rummage sale.

Mule-packing in the Sierras, 1937 (YOUNG)

The mule and the burro were considered pack stock, so all of us except Henry took turns riding and walking, using the ride-and-tie procedure. Henry towed the pack string from the deck of his recalcitrant steed. Henry wasn't much for walking, or talking.

Intermittent walking was less of a hardship than riding all the time for those of us who had not been on a horse for years. After our supplies dwindled, as they did at an appalling rate, and our real estate salesman had stiffened up from sleeping on the ground, we had to press the burro into service as a steed for him. That took some doing, not only to persuade the burro to make like Rocinantes, but also to load the rider for he was no lightweight. However, it was easier than getting him onto a horse, since the burro was built closer to the ground. It was also easier getting him off again, for all he had to do was to stand up as best he could and the burro would walk out from under.

It would have helped if any of us had ever been on a pack trip before, especially when it came to lashing the load on the mule. Since even Henry did not know a squaw hitch from a granny, we had a rough time the first few days, with the mlle managing to shuck off the pack every few miles. Then we met a young Indian at the head of a string of horses coming at breakneck speed down the trail.

He had to stop because we were in the way. He took in the situation at a glance, slid off his horse, and in half a dozen practiced motions made a perfect hitch on the mule load. We made a careful sketch to guide us in future efforts and after that had little more trouble, provided we remembered to deflate the mule with a firm knee in the ribs before cinching the girth or whatever it is that one cinches on a pack steed.

Even at this late date I find it humiliating to have to report that we were lost most of the time, despite good maps and early Boy Scout training, not to mention two or three compasses.

First off, the well-defined trail we were following ended suddenly in a hideous tangle of downed trees, dust and confusion somewhere on the western slope of the Sierras. We had run into a timber-cutting operation of the kind called "harvesting" but resembling a total disaster.

Amid the crashing of trees and the roaring of bulldozers, we finally located an angry-looking woodsman who told us to get the hell out of there, indicating the way by a wave of his hand. We took a wide detour that lasted all day before we found a trail which we hoped was the right one. It was one of the worst days I ever spent in the woods.

Late that evening, we arrived at a mountain homestead that sported a big haystack beside a shake-roofed log cabin and a gaggle of barking dogs. The rancher did not seem overjoyed to see us, but he did sell us some hay (at about a nickel a bite) and let us sleep in the haystack with the hounds to guard us.

The next morning we were off early, following directions the rancher gave us to reach a place called Cherry River. He said we could not miss it. He did not know us very well. We rode all day, evidently in a circle, for we wound up that evening back at the ranch.

This time the rancher was even less happy to see us, and I thought he was unduly ostentacious about shooing his two pretty teenage girls indoors as we rode up. He need not have worried; we were all asleep within seconds of hitting the hay and the entire Ziegfeld Follies chorus line could have pranced through our camp that night without causing an eyelid to quiver.

The next morning he saw us off again, but this time sent one of his sons along to escort us. Of course, finding the trail under those conditions was simple, even for us, and we reached Cherry River about noon. We could see fish in the clear water, so we went fishing. We were greenhorns enough to have counted on trout as part of our menu, and here was an obvious chance to fill our larder.

Let me dismiss that sorry subject here and now. We saw scores of fine, fat trout on our trip but caught exactly none. One of my more painful recollections is of dangling worms, grubs, small frogs, flies, spinner, salmon eggs, doughballs and hunks of cheese and combinations of those presumably irresistible goodies, right under the noses of cruising leviathans. They did not even deign to turn away from the distasteful sight, but merely closed their eyes and went back to sleep, while we went hungry.

Somewhere on the far side of Cherry River we got lost again, but did not worry about it since we were near timber line and could see forever. One day, while following a Forest Service trail we had stumbled upon, we were disconcerted to find it ending abruptly in a lake, surrounded by a large swamp.

After staring at the water a while, we realized that all the trees standing in the water were still alive, meaning that the lake was of recent origin and probably temporary.

Sure enough, we found the trail, leading straight out into the lake on a sort of stone causeway just under the surface. As there was no place else to go, we followed it. We had trouble at first getting our livestock to get their feet wet until I led my steed of the moment, that big and amiable Belgian mare, out onto the causeway. The rest followed.

That improbable path was too narrow to permit me to get back around the horse to mount, so I waded, leading the parade across a quarter mile of icy water almost to my knees. It was invigorating.

The trail led us over a tiny island no more than a hundred feet across. It had a topknot of gnarled spruce trees that hid a tent, and in the tent were resting a couple of honeymooners, or so we surmised. They said they had been fishing. They told us the water had risen about a foot in the past week, covering the trail. They said a packer was due to come for them in a few days and they had plenty of supplies. Obviously they had each other.

In retrospect, they did not seem any more glad to see us than the rancher had been. Anyhow, they did not invite us to supper.

After about a week on the trail, we were really getting low on food, but we were saved from eating our shoes by the discovery of a jar of jam and a whole package of biscuit flour in a box nailed to a tree in a deserted camp.

We dined royally that night on Dutch oven biscuits filled with jam, along with frogs' legs. We had found by accident that the reeds along many of the small lakes were full of bullfrogs of considerable size, and that they would snap at a red streamer fly intended for trout.

Filled with frogs' legs and well being, we decided to rest up a day in camp beside a lovely lake literally jumping with big trout. I was not going to mention fish again and have no reason to do so now, for the result was the same.

That night, for the first time, rain threatened. We persuaded Henry, our young wrangler, to move in with us under the shelter of a tarpaulin instead of sleeping out with the livestock as had been his custom. This was an error on three counts.

First, it did not rain. Second, the unattended animals scattered themselves all over the mountainside. Third, one or more of them came into camp and raided our meager remaining food supplies, which we had imprudently left out on an improvised camp table.

When we awakened, it was too late. Our flour was spread all over the ground, weevils and all, as was everything else that could be scattered. All we were able to salvage was about half a box of dried apricots, some coffee mixed with sand, and a few strips of dried cornmeal mush called polenta that even the burro would not eat.

We ate it because it was all we had for breakfast, and lunch too. At this point we got the message: we had to get out of the mountains, or starve. Our maps said it was about forty miles by trail back to our starting point, where we had left our cars, but only about twenty-five miles if we went directly across country. In view of our sorry record of getting lost on well-marked trails, this seemed downright silly, but we made it somehow.

About noon, after six hours of blindly following ridge tops in the general direction of our cars, we came out of the woods on an old logging track right where our topographic maps said it should be, at the bottom of a wide canyon. We followed it down to a junction with a graded road that looked well-traveled but was deep in red dust.

After another hour, we met some motorists. When the second or third car stopped to let the occupants snap pictures of us, and a small boy yelled, "Hey, Pop, look at all the bad guys," we began to realize what we looked like.

We were ragged, unshaven and drooping with fatigue, caked with dust and sweat from head to toe. We had tied bandanas over our faces not for any theatrical effect but to keep out some of the dust. We must have resembled a bunch of bandits from a hillbilly horse opera.

So we decided to make the most of the situation by tying all our hardware on the outside where it would show—a couple of holstered .22 pistols, a hatchet, some big hunting knives (for cleaning all those trout). Thus appropriately accoutered, we rode in late afternoon into a little mountain resort that was full of tourists and summer-home residents, all dressed up fit to kill (this was long before the jeans craze).

Amid the clatter of camera shutters, we tied our mounts to a hitching rail that looked as if it had never been used for that purpose before, hitched up our belts, pulled down our bandanas, and strode into the village cocktail lounge as if we owned the place. It was the Butch Cassidy gang coming into the Long Branch saloon to confront Matt Dillon.

Of course, we had to order shots of red-eye, which we had to translate to whiskey (on the rocks) for the benefit of the goggle-eyed youth behind the bar. The other patrons all left in a hurry, possibly because we must have been pretty powerful by then in our collective unwashed aura.

After a couple of rounds each on empty stomachs, we felt able to complete our journey of nine or ten miles down the highway, feeling no pain but hunger. Besides, we still had to get our rheumatic member into a car for a fast ride home as he was in pretty bad shape.

Since I lived near his home, I was elected to do the driving. Some thirty hours after being awakened by livestock in the larder, I completed my mission and went home to sleep for eighteen hours.

I thought then, and have thought many times since, that there has to be a better way to go on a pack trip. After reading the latest in brochures on the subject, I'm going to try it one of these days.

22

MISADVENTURE IN THE GROVES OF ACADEME

EDITORS AND EDUCATORS who deplore the present state of higher education in English, finding college students approaching functional illiteracy, may be cheered to learn that it was like that more than forty years ago.

As assistant city editor of the *San Jose Mercury Herald* in the late 1930s, I was invited to teach a course in country journalism at San Jose State one semester (and only one). At the time, it sounded like a splendid idea, since it offered a modest additional stipend. It was also something of an ego trip, since I had attended college only for a couple of years.

On the other hand, when I went into the newspaper game a decade earlier, journalism degrees were looked upon with scorn by the old hands. In fact, a youngster fresh out of J-school usually found it wise to keep quiet about his credentials. The preferred route to success was to start as a copyboy (or girl—now called a copyperson, I believe) and wait for a break.

By the end of the 1930s, however, the level of competence at San Jose State in the field of journalism had improved immeasurably since my college days, and I felt no qualms about joining the department as a visiting instructor for three hours a week. In fact, I felt flattered. I did not have sense enough to feel very nervous.

Up to that time, if I had thought about it at all, I had thought of teaching journalism as a sort of poor relation of the news profession. I believed that about all that was required was a solid background in the subject matter, which I imagined I had. Little did I know about the pitfalls and bear traps that lay hidden in the thickets of academia.

As I remember, sixteen students showed up for the opening session, thirteen men and three women. (They were all juniors and seniors, so I shall not call them boys and girls. They probably thought of me as a funny old man, at the age of thirty).

I recall only one of the men by name, which was Alex. He was undoubtedly in the genius category, and could have become a top-notch newspaperman or anything else he wanted to be. I learned, by chance, that he was working full time as a night orderly at Agnew State Hospital, while earning straight A's in a heavy schedule at school. I do not know when he slept. He sat erect in class with his eyes closed, but when I asked him a question he always had the correct answer at the tip of his tongue, and his written work was flawless. (Later, I heard that he had died from a brain tumor in his senior year, a tragic loss to society).

The three young women I also remember, not just because they were easy on the eyes, but because they were well versed in the uses of the language and could type better than I could. All three went into journalism after college, I believe.

The remaining twelve men were something else. I remember them as an amorphous mass of egregiously masculine beef, to me quite indistinguishable one from another, all tongue-tied. I did not find out until later how utterly nonverbal they were.

For starters, I lectured. I explained the differences between country (small-town) journalism and the art as it is practiced in big cities. In small-town newspapers, I told them, there is no insulation between the reporter or the editor (often the same person) and the reading public. Irate citizens can and often do storm the citadel to deal directly with the malefactor who mixed up the names in a wedding story.

Country journalism, I explained (using some personal encounters as examples) is personal journalism—there never is any question as to who is responsible for each and every item in the paper. Furthermore, quite often the citizens know more about the news behind the news than the editor does, unless he has lived there all his life.

Metropolitan newspapers, by comparison, are at the other end of the scale in journalism and not necessarily for the best. They seem cold and remote, with the news staff securely entrenched behind several layers of insulation. Big-city reporters can and do get away with stuff that in a small town would be an invitation to mayhem. As an example, a former employer of mine, John Tiedeman, then in his sixties, was severely beaten at his home by a committee of heroic war veterans who objected to an editorial in his Morgan Hill weekly paper, criticizing some sort of veterans' benefit. He was a retired army officer who had seen active service in World War I. While he was in the hospital, I moonlighted as his editor.

Back in the classroom, so long as I was doing all the talking, I got along fine. Then came the debacle.

Instead of a text, I had asked each of the students to subscribe or otherwise obtain the local weekly or daily newspaper from his or her hometown. For practice assignments, I had each rewrite a local news story, using imagination or personal knowledge to expand the article if possible.

For Alex and the three women, that was duck soup. For the other twelve it was a disaster, as it was for me. None of them could type, compose a complete sentence, or use punctuation in anything but shotgun fashion. If that is an exaggeration, it is not much of one.

I tried to explain that since this was an upper-division English course, I did not think I was being unreasonable when I expected some semblance of literacy, or that it was asking too much to require journalism students to turn in typewritten material. In my innocence or arrogance, I thought that anybody who signed up for a journalism class had some idea of going into the profession and some aptitude for it.

We wound up in quite a hassle. I finally agreed to a kind of compromise. I would give double grades, one over the other, on all written submissions. The top grade would represent journalistic enterprise and effort; the lower grade would be my evaluation of their use of English grammar, including spelling, punctuation, and what used to be called composition.

Of course, for Alex and the three women, it was A/A or at worst, B/A. But for the 12, I had to award grades like B/F if I was feeling charitable, or F/F if I was not. I continued to insist on typewritten papers, which must have been quite a burden for a dozen girl friends or sisters.

At the end of the course, I found I had no choice but to flunk the twelve, all of them. They did not seem unduly disturbed, having by that time, I now suspect, written me off as some sort of kook. I did not apply for another term as a visiting professor, nor was I invited.

You see, at the time I did not know I was dealing with a large segment of the football team, who had no more interest in journalism than they had in medieval Latin.

In retrospect, I realize now that I should have found that out the first day and suggested to the twelve that they seek elsewhere for easy credits. If they had, I would have wound up with a class enrollment of four, and my career as a teacher would have ended then and there, as it should have.

23

THE BARTENDER'S PARDON

THIS ALL HAPPENED long before Watergate, but in retrospect it has a family resemblance to some of the background of that event.

One night I had a telephone call on the city desk from a deputy sheriff who was the undercover source of some good stories from time to time. He started out by telling me not to mention his name but just to meet him right now in the alley behind the office. It sounded very cloak-and-daggerish but worth looking into, so I agreed.

The deputy (who might be called Deep-Throat since I have forgotten his name) was waiting in a car with the motor running and drove away as soon as I got in. After circling around a few times to make sure he was not followed, he stopped under the shade of a tree on a quiet side street. He then admonished me not ever to divulge the source of what he was about to tell me, or his job would be on the block, if not worse.

Now, after forty-odd years, the details and the sequence of the events have become hazy and I have no way to vertify the data, but this is what I recall:

A notorious bartender, whom I shall call Sam, had gone to prison for manslaughter as a result of a barroom brawl in which he banged a customer over the head with a shovel blade with fatal results.

Sam was supposed to be in the slammer on a five-to-ten-year sentence, but now, according to the deputy, he was out after only about a year behind San Quentin's unlovely walls. Furthermore, he was out on a pardon and not on a parole. That much I could verify and did so with a telephone call to the bar as soon as I returned to the office. Yep, good old Sam was back at the bar setting up drinks for all and sundry, but he was not telling how he got there. We then had a council of war in the city room, for we knew we had a very hot potato on our hands.

What came next in the deputy's account was not so easy to verify. In fact, for us at the time it was downright impossible. The pardon, the deputy said, had been purchased by one or more prominent businessmen, but for what reason the deputy did not know. Perhaps, he said, Sam knew where a lot of bodies were buried.

From whom had it been purchased and how? From the governor's secretary, according to the deputy. The secretary was making a mint on the side by slipping blank pardon forms into the stacks of stuff he had ready for the governor to sign, and that was that. The good governor was much too busy getting ready for his next county fair appearance, or whatever, to bother about reading all those papers.

But how were we ever going to cash in on this journalistic gold mine? The governor, as well as the prominent local businessmen involved, were all staunch Republicans. Our publishers, I think, firmly believed that all Republicans sat at the right hand of God while Democrats lurked down at the other place with the Socialists and Communists and others who never washed their necks.

Also, in its existing form the story was pure libel. Then somebody had a bright idea. We called the Associated Press in Sacramento, where we got in touch with a former San Jose newsman we all knew and fed him the story. He promised to follow up and did so with dispatch.

The next day he phoned to tell us that the governor's secretary was already under indictment by a grand jury for his pardon-selling enterprise, but that the story somehow had been hushed up under extreme pressure from the state house. The Associated Press, immune to such pressure, got it out on our tip and was putting it on the wires that evening.

Now we were obliged, under our circumstances at the time, to let our publishers know about the story (but not how it had been discovered) before printing it. Needless to say, there was instant consternation on the part of the publishers.

At first they flatly refused to believe the story. Then they did not want us to print it at all. Only after we assured them that it would be on the front pages of all the papers in the state, if not the nation, including our circulation rivals, did they grudgingly agree to let us use the story—on an inside page under an innocuous heading. It was a victory of sorts, I suppose, but we all felt a little sick when we saw the banner headlines in the San Francisco papers.

Needless to say also, the anonymous role of the local businessmen was not mentioned. The governor's secretary went to prison and the governor, doubtless an innocent dupe in the matter, did not seek re-election. I never heard what became of Sam.

24

THE GOLDEN TROUT OF SALLY KEYES

THE SECOND SUMMER after we were married, while I was still working at the *Mercury Herald,* Emma Lou and I undertook a private pack trip into the California Sierras, something we had wanted to do for a long time, talked about it endlessly, and finally saved up enough money and vacation time to do it. It turned out to be a great and at times painful adventure for a pair of city-dwelling tenderfeet. The time was August, 1939.

I do not remember just how we happened to pick Blaney Meadows as our destination, but I assume somebody had told us about the place and had said it was not too hard to get to. In the Sierra Club bulletin we found the name of a packer and wrote to him for a date. He responded by return mail, and we were off and running.

The packer told us to meet him on the west side of Florence Lake, near the boat landing, on the appointed day. Florence Lake was then, as it is now, the edge of the wilderness east of Fresno, about twenty-five miles beyond Huntington Lake where the highway ends.

I remember that road very well, for it was by all odds the worse piece of rocky trail I had ever taken a passenger car over, consisting of a rough, steep, crooked, one-lane construction trail with few turnouts. The trip took us nearly seven hours.

Come to think of it, I had been over the first part of the route a few years before on a fishing trip, but had turned back at the top of Kaiser Pass because the road beyond looked so bad. I recall the spot because it was there I met my first rattlesnake face to face. The serpent was curled around the base of the signpost that read: KAISER PASS—Elev. 9195 ft. Anyone in the Sierras will tell you that rattlers are never found above 7,000 feet. So that one must have been lost, or the sign was wrong.

When we arrived at the lake shore, nobody was in sight, and there was no sign of a pack train. However, down the shore a little way we saw a tent. In it, we found a woman crying. She said she was the wife, or rather the widow, of the packer. He had died of a ruptured appendix a few days before while taking a party into the region where we were heading, and she had just that day returned from the funeral.

Since I still had an appendix which had kicked up a fuss on a few occasions, I began to feel some qualms about the trip. But the good lady rallied and said she would take us in the next day because she needed the money, but she was short of pack stock and one of us would have to walk.

She rode, leading a pack horse loaded with our belongings, while Emma Lou and I took turns riding the remaining horse. We did not mind this arrangement since we were both far more accustomed to walking to riding, and we found that we could cut off the first four miles by taking a boat across the lake for one dollar each.

The lady met us at the other side, and that afternoon, seven miles farther on, left us and our equipment in a pleasant grove of tall, skinny pines in the middle of Blaney Meadows, on the icy south fork of the San Joaquin river. It was a lovely camping spot with ample firewood, requiring only that we put up a fence of readily available pine piles to keep out wandering livestock. So far as we could see, we were entirely alone.

There we loafed for several days, getting use to the altitude, the solitude, and the peace. We were entertained by the antics of several squirrels, a pair of camp-robbing Canada jays, and busy bunches of pigmy nuthatches. We had been warned to keep food like bacon and meat out of the reach of bears and racoons, and we did so by slinging a sack on a rope between two trees, but we saw no sign of marauders of any species all the time we were there.

We did a little fishing, and even took some dips in the river, a madly rushing, waist-deep torrent coming right off a glacier. It was more like surfing than swimming—we jumped into the river and it spewed us out on a sandbar a hundred yards downstream, only a few seconds before we turned to ice. It was, to say the least, invigorating. In between jumps we thawed out in the sun, watching juncos and rosy finches and nutcracker crows in the trees right over our heads. It was obvious the place was seldom visited, for the birds showed no fear of our presence.

One day we met an old hermit who came by looking for a lost horse. He said he had a summer cabin a few miles up the river. He told us about the fabulous golden trout in the Sally Keyes lakes which he said were "not far" from our camp, how to get there, and how to catch the fish (using a big streamer fly on a colorado spinner). He said nobody had been up to the lakes for several years, so far as he knew.

On our map, "not far" appeared to be about six miles, so the next day we casually packed some lunch and our fishing tackle and set out for a stroll up to the lakes. We were green enough not to know that mountain miles often are about three times as long as miles on the level. The route turned out to be almost straight up a switchback trail ascending the face of a bare granite cliff face with no shade whatever, to an elevation of 11,500 feet.

If we had had the sense to leave camp at first light, we might have made the climb before the day became too hot. As it was with our midmorning start, we were exposed to the full blast of the incredibly bright mid-August High Sierra sun the entire distance, and we fried. I will never know why we did not both die of heat exhaustion.

Nor will I ever know how or why we managed to complete that climb. I recall only too well that we would count ten steps out loud and then fall down; get up, count ten more steps, and fall down again. When we finally staggered over the rim, we were both too far gone to pay much attention to the beauty of the scene—a series of saucerlike ponds scooped out of the glaciated granite at timber line, tiered one above the other like a huge Japanese garden, fringed with lodgepole pines no more than ten feet high, standing dark and somber against the glittering granite slopes of the snow peaks all around us.

Emma Lou and I both collapsed under a tree and fell asleep in an instant. An hour or so later I revived enough to crawl around and gather some sticks for a little fire and brewed some tea in a tin cup. After several cups of the hot brew to wash down a couple of sandwiches, I limped down to the shore of the nearest pond to look for the famous fish.

The water did not look inviting. It was murky, like most glacier-fed lakes, and the bottom near the shore was strewn with moss-covered logs. However, I had nothing else to do so I followed the old hermit's directions and tossed a spinner-fly combination out onto the pond.

Now this is not a fish story and I will not belabor the details. Suffice it to say that in the next twenty or thirty minutes I pulled in half a dozen of the most beautiful trout I had ever seen, all a uniform fourteen inches long, weighing perhaps a pound and a half apiece. Their backs were gray, making them invisible in the water, but their undersides were flaming red-gold that flashed in the sun when they turned to strike at the lure.

Out on the grassy bank they were even more spectacular in appearance, more like huge goldfish in an aquarium than wild trout in an alpine tarn. When Emma Lou awoke and saw them, she thought they were all bleeding.

I stopped fishing when I had six trout, partly because I thought I had reached the legal weight limit (ten pounds and one fish), and partly because I had used up all my spare tackle on fish I could not land, or on snags. Besides, I had all the weight I wanted to lug back down that steep trail.

Going down was not so bad as coming up because it was cooler (we waited until sundown to start), and we were losing altitude. But every downward step racked our knees and aching thighs and pushed our bruised and blistered toes farther through the holes in our socks. We knew then, if we ever did, the full meaning of the word "tenderfoot."

We recovered in a day or two, meanwhile finding our fish a welcome addition to our dwindling larder. Inexperienced as we were, we found we had underestimated our appetites and were running low on food ahead of schedule; but we still had time and food enough for one more small adventure we had planned.

This one involved a longer hike than the one to the Sally Keyes lakes, but was at lower altitude, through the trees and on more or less level terrain. Also, we left camp shortly after dawn, long before the sun climbed over the rim, when the dew still glistened on the grass and the robins were starting to chirp their sleepy morning greetings.

We had no marked trail to follow, but merely walked along the bank of the river upstream through mixed woodland and open country about eight miles to a place where a suspension bridge offered the only crossing of the river for fifty miles—or so we were assured by our copy of Walter Starr's *Guide to the John Muir Trail.*

We also had with us a copy of the Sierra Club's summer high-trip itinerary and from it could calculate that the club's 200 or more hikers and their supply train would be crossing that bridge at about noon that day and we intended to be there.

We figured it just right—we strolled across the bridge at high noon on the heels of the pack train, to the obvious astonishment of the entire party. They had seen no other people in nearly two weeks and had not expected to meet anyone out there in the far back of beyond. A dozen or so members of the party who were also friends of ours from home were even more flabbergasted over our sudden appearance, for we had told no one of our plans.

When they all demanded to know how we happened to be there and where we had come from, we replied casually that we had been out for a morning walk and had stopped by for lunch. All in all it was well worth the effort of the all-day hike.

A few days later, realizing we had no alternative unless we were to go hungry soon, we walked out to Florence Lake early one morning, luckily arriving there just as a boat came in bringing supplies to a camping party on the east shore. We sent a message to our packer asking her to come and get us as soon as possible. Then we scrounged some potatoes and carrots from the other campers to make a stew with a hunk of tough dried beef we had and hiked back to camp, hoping our message would get through and that the lady would come for us before we had to eat our shoelaces.

She arrived at noon the next day, but minus still another steed, so Emma Lou and I both had to walk out, not only to the lake but on around it since we had missed the daily boat trip. It was not so much the eleven or twelve miles we had to hike, as we were in pretty good shape by then, but the heat and the dust that did us in. All we had strength enough to do, after we had loaded our gear into our car and paid the packer ($35), was to point the nose of the car downhill and hope it remembered the way.

I will never forget the denouement of that part of the drama. We arrived on the outskirts of Fresno after midnight, much too tired and sleepy to go another mile. We stopped at the first auto court we came to, a dreary-looking gaggle of unpainted shacks. (Auto courts in the 1930s were in general pretty grim, a far cry from today's posh caravansaries, and this one was no exception).

However the price was right, the beds proved to be free of bugs (we looked), and the place had a shower and a kitchen of sorts, so we paid the fee to the slovenly proprietor and moved in. While Emma Lou heated up some cans of food we had left in the car, I peeled off for a shower, full of keen anticipation.

Out came a feeble trickle of rusty cold water. I don't know when I have been more profoundly disappointed. We thought of rousing the inkeeper, but realized the futility of that gesture and made do by taking turns pouring over each other pans of water heated on the stove. Then we swallowed some food, fell into bed, and did not wake up until noon the next day. I had to go back to work the following afternoon, but it was a week before we fully recovered from that vacation.

25

E. J. DEMSON

RUMORS WERE MORE RAMPANT than usual at the old *San Jose Mercury Herald* in the early months of 1941, and that is saying a lot, for it seems to me that newspapers have always been fertile breeding grounds for rumors. These whisperings, however, were different—they pertained to things imminent and drastic.

One batch said the newspaper was about to go broke. We had been hearing this for years and paid the rumors little heed.

Another bunch of gossip said the paper was about to be combined with the rival *San Jose Evening News,* perhaps under a new owner. We did not believe that one either, although it turned out to be true.

For all the variety of reports, not a one predicted the first actual event in the earthshaking (for us) series that started up abruptly that spring.

One day, out of the blue, suddenly appeared a remarkable character by the name of E. J. Demson, in the guise of general manager, a catchall title that included, as we were to discover, the role of editor in chief. That illustrious position had been vacant

The old Mercury Herald *offices on W. Santa Clara* (SAN JOSE HISTORICAL MUSEUM)

for years. A financial expert as well as an attorney, Demson specialized in newspaper finance. He had been sent out by a client, a Cleveland bank, to look over the *Mercury Herald* as a candidate for a loan of considerable size.

It did not take him long to discover that the newspaper was on shaky financial ground, and to report back to the bank that he could not recommend it as a good risk. For some reason I never could pin down, however, he decided to take a shot at putting the paper back on its feet financially, on his own. I suspect he might have been inspired by a comparison between the climates of Cleveland and San Jose, plus a desire to get out of the Cleveland rat race. Or perhaps he had always wanted to run a small-town newspaper, and San Jose in 1941 was still a small town at heart, for all its near-metropolitan size. In retrospect, I am not at all certain that his motives were entirely clear to Demson himself.

He took the newspaper by the scruff of the neck and shook it as a big dog would a rat, and the fleas fell out in flocks, along with a lot of loose fur.

From what little I could piece together from the fragments he let slip, he must have been about forty-five years old at the time. He said he was never sure of his birthdate, since his parents brought him to this country very early in life and left all records behind. They were refugees from Austria, I recall his saying. He was in the U.S. Army with Pershing in Mexico during the pursuit of Pancho Villa in 1916, and in the Air Force in World War II, but in what capacity I do not know.

All I do know for certain is what I remember of what he did while he was in charge of the *Mercury Herald* for about ten months in 1941, and perhaps his ideas and his deeds describe him better than biographical details. In modern parlance, Demson was something else. He was directly responsible for the most extraordinary ten months I ever spent in the newspaper game, or anywhere else for that matter.

At first, while the rumor factory operated at close to the speed of light, Demson busied himself in familiar territory, downstairs where the profits were supposed to come from. He fired both the business manager and the advertising manager and brought in a new circulation manager to fill a long-standing vacancy.

Next he strolled into the editorial department and all hell broke loose. It was not so much what he did, at first, but the ideas he espoused, that shook the sacred pillars.

He let it be known that he had a curious notion about who owned the newspaper. Obviously, the owners owned the plant, the circulation list, and the good will, such as it was. But, he said, the owners of the plant did not own the space in the newspaper's pages. The advertising space had been sold to the advertisers, to use as they wished within reason and the bounds of decency.

The space left for news, in his view, belonged to the subscribers. They had paid for that space, he said, and it was his job and the responsibility of the editorial people to see that the space was filled with news and not propaganda.

These ideas were, of course, straight heresy just short of fantasy. I think the publishers must have been waiting for Jehovah to send down a lightning bolt to strike him dead in his Number Twelves. None of us, however, believed all this was anything more than hot air, or wishful thinking, having categorized Demson as a fast-talking con artist. We soon found out he was prepared to back up his bluff.

Next he abolished business-office "musts," those shibboleths of most editors. They were free blurbs disguised as news items handed out by the advertising department as rewards for big ads.

Then he put a ban on any and all publicity stories unless they had news value in the judgment of the editorial staff. That edict went over like a lead balloon with the service clubs and other organizations used to getting unpaid plugs for their turkey shoots. The ban led to some quite lively publicity stunts—like the time the Norse-American society staged a sham battle between two Vikings in full armor in the middle of the main intersection at high noon on a Saturday. The traffic was backed up for blocks in all directions and the Vikings went to jail, but they made the front page, with photos.

Next he issued a notice to the staff that henceforth no free tickets to any entertainment would be accepted—not any at all. He set up a slush fund for reporters to draw on when they had to buy tickets for some event they were assigned to cover—a prize fight, a football game, a theatrical event.

It was worth the price of admission to see the look of utter consternation on the faces of the PR people and the front men for circuses, shows, fights, games and all manner of commercial entertainment where free press passes had been in vogue for generations.

Some of the reporters did not like it either. I do not think the phrase "conflict of interest" had crept into common usage back then, but clearly that is what Demson had in mind and he was entirely correct. Reporters who accepted gratuities in any form from anyone they might have to write about were being bought and paid for, like some Congressmen. They had no place in Demson's scheme of things.

The cynics on the copy desk, unbelievers to the end, took all this as showmanship, and sat back to wait for the crunch which was sure to come when Demson's weird policies ran headlong into a major advertiser's desires. It was not long in happening.

One night a delegation from the newly formed Montgomery Ward employees' union showed up in the office with an announcement that a strike vote had just been taken. It was news, and we ran it, fully aware that it was without a doubt the first time such an item of labor news had ever appeared in the columns of that arch-conservative bulwark of the Establishment.

The next morning the local manager of the store cancelled all his advertising in the *Mercury Herald* and switched it over to the *News.* That could have been a fatal step, for the *Mercury Herald,* since the big department stores and their lucrative advertising budgets were all that stood between any newspaper and bankruptcy.

If the other big stores followed the lead of Montgomery Ward, the paper was doomed.

That bit of brinkmanship did not seem to faze Demson at all. He countered with a front-page editorial—another sensational first—blasting the store's manager for attempting to abridge the First Amendment to the Constitution. He waved the flag, the Bible, motherhood, and apple pie, everything but the Easter bunny. Then he fired off a copy by airmail special delivery to the president of Montgomery Ward, in Chicago.

I do not remember exactly what happened next, but it seems to me that in less than two days Montgomery Ward was clamoring to get its advertising back into the *Mercury Herald,* and that Demson, who had a puckish sense of humor, kept the store out of the paper for a week in penance. I wish I had kept a copy of that editorial—it was a blockbuster for sure.

After that episode it was no holds barred in the news room. We dug up stories that blasted the Republicans one day, the Democrats the next, labor unions the following, and so on. One politician told me he was afraid *not* to read the paper the first thing every morning to see whether his number had come up.

The word got around. A state health inspector came in to complain that he had been trying to shut down an abortion parlor that had been running for years on end in a fashionable part of town, with a sorry record for postoperative infections. He said he had been unable to get any help from the local police.

Demson called the chief of police and laid down the law to him, to the effect that he (the chief) was about to stage a raid on the parlor that very night, and that no advance word of the raid had better leak out to anyone, including the lady in charge.

It didn't, and the raid was a complete success (from the point of view of the state health official and the newspaper). We ran the pictures our photographer took of the flabbergasted old madam telling her beads with tears running down her face—ran them two columns wide the whole length of the front page. We provided the address, which was across the street from the junior high school in one of the more exclusive residential areas of the city.

That tour de force cost us some subscribers among the gentry, who thought it all in bad taste, but we were gaining new ones so fast by that time we didn't mind losing a few in a good cause. By then any attempt by anyone (including the publishers, as it turned out) to suppress a legitimate news story was tantamount to guaranteeing front-page coverage.

One day, not long before Pearl Harbor, Demson received a letter from an old friend, who was high up in the Navy hierarchy in Washington, labeled confidential and secret and all that jazz. It said that a British cruiser was being repaired in the Navy's big Mare Island shipyard in San Francisco Bay and that the Navy wanted it kept quiet. Presumably this was to keep the information from getting to the German embassy's exceedingly competent spy ring in San Francisco. If the Germans didn't already know all about the cruiser, they would have had to been asleep, for something like 2500 British tars were running around the bay region with *H.M.S. Liverpool* emblazoned in gold letters on the front of their funny little flat hats.

We knew about them but had not been aware there was supposed to be anything secret about their presence. In fact, a whole bunch of them were scheduled to march in uniform in an Armistice Day parade right there in San Jose a few days hence.

This situation obviously was right up our alley. We got in touch with the managing editor of the Vallejo paper, right next door to Mare Island, and found, as we had suspected, that they had a whole set of nice photos of the cruiser but had been afraid to run them in the face of a Navy ban. However, if we would take the lead, they would follow, the editor said.

The cruiser, as it turned out, had had its front end blown off in the battle of Malta, or some such place, and had been towed backwards around the world to reach Mare Island, the only safe harbor with docks and equipment for such a huge repair job. No more than 10,000 people had seen it come in. It was a sensational story, but it had never seen the light of day until then. I never did learn how the Navy had succeeded in muzzling all four San Francisco dailies, not to mention a couple in Oakland, since the whole event was about as secret as a Rose Bowl game.

Vallejo sent us a bunch of photos and we made up several pages and rushed a set of stereo mats by motorcycle messenger back to Vallejo on the same night that we were to run them in the *Mercury Herald.* As soon as we phoned that our presses were running with the spread, the Vallejo morning paper followed suit.

The expected Navy entourage, headed by an admiral in full gold-braid glory, blew into the editorial department the next afternoon. Demson, with a ceremonial flourish, brought them all out to the city room to be introduced.

At the city desk, Demson said that the Navy wanted to know why we had seen fit to ignore the Navy's ban on the story and had given it such full treatment. He was very stern and poker-faced. Equally poker-faced and exuding proper concern, I earnestly assured the admiral that we had only carried out Demson's order to print the news and added that it really was not much of a secret anyhow.

The admiral got red around the gills, but he knew when he was licked and simply turned on his heel and stalked out followed by his flunkies. I suspected at the time that he did not have his heart in his mission but was merely carrying out orders. I guess the Navy was not too upset with Demson over the incident, for he joined the Navy himself a few months later.

26

CRUSADES

I AM SURE we made our share of errors with our brash policy at the *Mercury,* tilted many windmills, went on feckless crusades and were embarrassed from time to time: one night we went to press with a story that the city council was going to fire the city manager; it didn't; and the opposition paper rubbed our noses in it.

Given our new-found freedom, it was perhaps only natural that we should go overboard now and then, like a herd of colts turned loose in a field after long confinement in a barn. It took just one sad experience, however, to convince me that crusades went out of style in the 13th century and should have been left there.

Our Gilroy staff writer, Paul Conroy (later executive editor of the *Mercury News*) reported one day that a young girl was dying of pneumonia in her home but her parents, religious zealots, did not believe in doctors and medicine and refused to let her be treated.

A local doctor who had been smuggled into the room by neighbors made a snap diagnosis of pneumonia in the last stages. The neighborhood was up in arms over the situation. We at the

Mercury Herald organized a campaign to try to save the girl's life, exhibiting zeal to match that of the parents, but in the opposite direction. I would like to think that our motivations were purely humanitarian, but I am afraid we had one eye on headline possibilities.

In any event, almost at once we discovered that we really had ripped the lid off Pandora's box this time. It is not surprising, in view of the complications, that my memory of the rapid-fire events that followed were quite confused, and remained so until Paul Conroy sent me some clippings he had saved.

The highly involved story is perhaps best told in a chronology written at the time by George Challis, one of the team of reporters we had turned loose on the scene. Here it is, under a dateline of June 18, 1941:

9 A.M. (Monday) Dr. D. L. Morse of Gilroy phoned Judge Leon Thomas to inform him that Louise Ford, 14, was seriously ill and the family refused medical aid.

10 A.M. After talking to the parents, Judge Thomas notified District Attorney John P. Fitzgerald and asked his aid. He went to Gilroy presumably to investigate.

6 P.M. The *Mercury Herald* called Fitzgerald at his home. He said he had been in Gilroy all day. "There isn't a thing I can do," he said, "It's a religious proposition. There's no law in the land that gives us authority to take a child from its parents."

6:25 P.M. The *Mercury Herald* phoned Superior Judge William F. James, juvenile court judge, at his Palo Alto home. Upon hearing the details, Judge James said a signed petition would have to be received by the county clerk's office and brought to him before he could issue a warrant ordering medical attention for the child. He said he would be available at his home all night.

6:50 P.M. Photographer Loris Gardner (doubling as a reporter) went to the county detention home to meet Mrs. Bessie McDonald, the juvenile probation officer, who had hurried from her Santa Clara residence to fill out the paper.

6:55 P.M. The *Mercury Herald* called Sheriff William J. Emig to ask for assistance in relaying the papers around the county. He was not available.

7:20 P.M. Phoned by Gardner, Judge James said it would be necessary for the county clerk, or a deputy, receive the signed petition and that it would be necessary for the physician to be on hand when the warrant was served. The judge said he would be at a lecture during the evening, but "there will be plenty of time."

7:45 P.M. Gardner left for Gilroy with the papers, accompanied by Deputy County Clerk Edmund T. McGeehee.

7:45 P.M. At the same time, the *Mercury Herald* reached Sheriff Emig, who agreed to send Deputy Elmer Moore with a fast car.

7:55 P.M. Deputy Moore and reporter Challis headed for Gilroy at 85 miles an hour.

8:22 P.M. In Gilroy, Judge Thomas signed the petition and Deputy Clerk McGeehee received it.

8:29 P.M. The sheriff's car headed north to Judge James' residence with the signed petition. Gardner remained in Gilroy to help Conroy arrange for a doctor, ambulance, hospital room and nurse for the girl—at the *Mercury's* expense.

9:40 P.M. Just 41 minutes after leaving Gilroy 50 miles to the south, the sheriff's party arrived at Judge James' home. He was not there and the housekeeper did not know how to reach him. A neighbor said the judge might be at a lecture hall at Stanford. The group went to the hall, had the judge paged without success. They went to the judge's home to wait for two hours.

11:10 P.M. George Challis phoned Superior Judge Robert R. Syer at his San Jose home to see if he would sign the warrant. During the conversation, Judge James arrived home.

11:41 P.M. Judge James signed the warrant, ordering that the child be given medical attention, then having Moore and McGeehee witness the signing. That took 25 minutes.

11:42 P.M. The party left for San Jose, dropped McGeehee,

picked up two more sheriff's deputies, then headed south with siren screaming and red light flashing.

12:30 A.M. (Tuesday) The sheriff's car ran out of gas on the outskirts of Gilroy, coasted into a service station. Gassed up, it had to be pushed by another car to start.

12:35 A.M. The car arrived at Hotel Milias, where a doctor was waiting with Conroy, Gardner, the ambulance and its crew. They all went at once to the child's home, where the doctor examined the girl and recommended that she be removed to Wheeler hospital at once. (For the next seven hours she was treated in vain.)

7:30 A.M. The child died.

There were repercussions, to be sure—an autopsy, an inquest, some angry editorials in newspapers, none of which did Louise Ford any good. Her parents said it was all the will of God.

Paul Conroy reported that his efforts on behalf of the *Mercury Herald,* endorsed by Judge Thomas, to promote public subscriptions to help defray funeral expenses, got a chilly reception in Gilroy. The funeral home donated its services and a handful of residents and business firms donated money, but the general attitude of the public seemed to be that the *Mercury Herald* had tried a publicity stunt that backfired.

Perhaps they were right. Good intentions seem to pave the same road for newspaper editors as they do for anyone else.

We had been involved a couple of years earlier with another Gilroy story that overnight became a sensation, for a while, with little or no assistance on our part and a somewhat happier ending.

One dull-news day in March, 1939, the *Mercury Herald* (along with hundreds of other newspapers) received a routine request from the Associated Press for any odds and ends of feature news for the weekend budget of filler copy. They didn't want spot news so much as timeless oddball material to keep the hungry teletypes fed.

About the only item we had that might fill the bill was a brief piece that Paul Conroy, our Gilroy staff writer, had sent in a day or so earlier. It was about a sidehill down in the southern end of the county that was slipping and seemed to be headed for a high-tension power line, a highway bridge, and a creek. It had the state highway department worried.

We called it the "Moving Mountain" and made a little play on the fact that it was in the so-called Dead Hills (Lomerias Muertas) and forgot about it, for the moment. But the Associated Press must have been hard up for news, or else there was a guy with a lively imagination on the rewrite desk, for the story bounced back on the teletype in considerably expanded form. The San Francisco papers seized upon it with joy and plastered it all over their front pages. Back on the *Mercury Herald,* we found ourselves hoist by our own petard, or anyhow scooped in our own back yard, in a manner of speaking.

We did not do too badly with the story ourselves, the next day, a Saturday, with some good reporting by Conroy and a four-column photo spread on the front page under a heading that read:

STRANGE SLIDE CHURNS PEACEFUL PASTURE

At least, somebody had a turn for alliteration on the copy desk. But we were counting on the Sunday paper, in which there always was much more room for picture displays, to do the story full justice as we reckoned its worth. Saturday night, however, the San Jose vocational high school burned down in a sensational fire and took over the front page of the Sunday paper, so the Moving Mountain moved back to the first page of the second section (where it actually belonged newswise).

The next thing we knew the good old general public, with assistance from the Associated Press, had decided it was a much bigger story than the so-called experts on the *Mercury Herald* had judged it to be. Highway 101 south of Gilroy was jammed for miles with curiosity seekers and amateur photographers; the highway patrol had to call out its reserves to handle the traffic.

Newspaper cameramen and newsreel photographers arrived

to record the scene for posterity. It would have been a natural for TV live coverage, had there been any TV in those innocent days.

The sidehill kept on slipping, a foot or so a day, bringing down acres of mud, rocks, shattered oak trees and thickets of poison oak. A brand-new gulch of large proportions came into being right before the eyes of the beholders, who swarmed all over the place in search of vantage points. The beleaguered ranch owner sent his mounted riders out to patrol the perimeter and to try to save his fences, but they were hopelessly outnumbered from the start.

I do not remember just how long that freakish story did actually last, but it was long enough for expert opinions and counter-opinions to be offered by various authorities. Numerous ideas for stemming the avalanche (we called it an "earth glacier" in one account) were made, but all of them were hopeless. In the end the Maving Mountain got tired and went to sleep. It was well short of the power line, the highway bridge, and the creek. The crowds got tired, too, and went home, leaving a sorely trampled pasture and a lot of broken fences for the bewildered ranch owner to mend.

At one point a university seismologist was called in to examine the slip and voiced an opinion that it might be the result of a little tremor on a branch of an old earthquake fault, but nobody gave the suggestion much attention, at the time.

Now we know that the so-called Hollister branch of the San Andreas fault runs right down through that part of the Santa Clara Valley. In fact, a fairly large quake did some damage there quite recently (1979). The San Andreas fault, of course, is the deep-seated fracture in the earth's crust that produced the 1906 tremblor that wrecked San Francisco and other towns from Santa Rosa to Hollister.

Nowadays it is known that along the fault in the region south of Gilroy almost constant but usually imperceptible motion is in progress, called "creep." Close to Hollister an old winery is slowly being torn apart by this action, and it has been listed as a National Natural Landmark by the Department of the Interior. Within the city limits of Hollister, some curbs and sidewalks are constantly being cracked by the same inexorable action.

No doubt it was just this sort of action that produced the sidehill slide, or earth slump as the seismologists term it. I shudder to think what the metropolitan papers would have done with *that* information had they known about it at the beginning. For that matter, I wonder what *we* might have done with it at the *Mercury Herald,* had it not been for the high school fire and our rather advanced state of ignorance in all matters scientific at the time.

27

LAST DAYS AT THE MERCURY

GETTING BACK to E. J. Demson and his revolutionary ideas, I can see now how our exceedingly active pursuit of the principle of printing the news and damning the torpedos was our own undoing, and Demson's. On the other hand, his number probably was up anyhow for a variety of reasons.

While I never heard Demson utter a word of criticism of the newspaper's publishers or the country-club crowd, the latter were not so inhibited when it came to discussing Demson. I heard from several sources that he was regarded as a parlor pink at the bare minimum, a wild-eyed menace to the Establishment and a collaborator with Harry Bridges at the worst.

I was probably included in the same category since I was without a doubt Demson's trained seal on the city desk, and a staunch supporter of the American Newspaper Guild to boot. The funny part of it was that we were both registered Republicans.

I remember quite well the incident that may well have been the one that fractured the camel, so to speak.

One of the two venerable old patriarchs who owned the paper

came to the city desk one afternoon to tell me he had just had a telephone call from the major of a nearby small town. This gentleman, according to the publisher, had been falsely accused of having in his possession an illegal number of undersized clams and had been unjustly hauled into court by a game warden for the picadillo.

He (the mayor) had asked the publisher not to run the story and naturally the publisher had agreed. The mayor, I believe, was chairman of the Republican County Central Committee at the time.

Not having heard of the story up to that time, I called our correspondent in that town and learned that he had seen the story on the front page of the local weekly paper, but had been told by the mayor that the *Mercury Herald* had agreed not to run it. I got the details from the weekly paper's publisher, a retired San Francisco newspaperman who knew a good story when he saw it.

He said the mayor had been sentenced and fined in justice court but the sentence had been suspended. The local sportsman's club, however, took a dim view of the proceedings and read the culprit out of the club, of which he had been an active member. Apparently the mayor had not bothered to mention this fact to the *Mercury Herald* publisher.

Now I was in a quandry. If I backed away from this one, all our noble gestures about printing the news, etc., would be so much gas. If I ran the story, even on the thin excuse that the mayor had not told the truth, I would be in direct violation of an order from the owner. If I went back to the owner, I felt sure the answer would still be a flat refusal, and it would stick.

So I took the matter to Demson. He listened, smiled his Cheshire cat smile and said, "Your decision."

He knew damned well what I would do, what I felt I had to do. I wrote the story and put it on page one. That night when I got home I told my wife I thought I had just cut my throat, figuratively speaking. As it happened, my prediction was premature.

Shortly after I arrived at the office the next day, I was summoned to The Presence, which consisted of the entire Family, and

Demson, gathered in the third-floor library reserved for such august occasions. It was called the library but it had no books in it, just a long table with high-backed, uncomfortable chairs around it.

One of the younger members of the Family, a San Francisco attorney whom I had encountered before during Guild negotiations, opened the ball. He did not invite me to sit down.

Had I or had I not received instructions from his father about killing a story about the mayor and his clams, he asked. I said I had.

Then, he continued pleasantly, could I tell the assemblage how the story happened to appear on the front page of the paper that morning?

I said I had put it there.

He asked why.

I recited the details, including the mayor's withheld information about the sportsman's club action and the fact that it had been on the front page of the weekly paper, and added that I felt I had no choice.

"Are we to understand that we cannot tell you what not to put into this newspaper?" the attorney asked with a bit of Perry Mason in his tone.

I said that was the case, since I felt I could take orders only from one boss at a time, and I had my orders from Mr. Demson to print the news at any cost.

"Did Mr. Demson know what you were doing with this story?" was the next question.

I looked at Demson down at the other end of the table. He sat there with his hands behind his head smiling at me. I smiled back.

"Not in detail, just in principle," I replied.

"We have no option in these matters, in your opinion?" asked the attorney.

"Oh, sure you have," I answered. "You can always fire me, and I suppose Mr. Demson too, if it comes to that."

Nobody seemed to have anything else to say, so I excused myself and went back to work, assuming that I still had a job for a little while. As a matter of fact nothing happened, and I finally left under my own power a couple of months later.

After the upstairs meeting, Demson strolled into the news room an hour or so later. He did not look ruffled, but then he never did. He said nothing about what had gone on after I left.

"You make it tough," he said.

I nodded. While neither of us ever mentioned the incident again, we both knew we had had it, in the long run. If it had not been that story, it would have been another one, for the world in general and San Jose in particular were not ready yet for the E. J. Demson brand of freewheeling journalism. But it was fun while it lasted, even though it made it just about impossible for me to stay in the newspaper game, as it turned out.

I must confess that I had not made my Quixotic gesture of defiance to the Establishment without some insurance. I knew, and they did not, that newspaper jobs were by then a dime a dozen, since so many newsmen had gone off to war or into war-related jobs. I had only to pick up the phone to line up another situation, and did so.

Demson left the paper shortly before I did, just after the *Mercury Herald* and its archrival combined and new owners of the two papers appeared on the scene. Demson and I later were associated in a couple of other enterprises, but that is another story.

28

"DAY OF INFAMY"

THE LAST MAJOR NEWS STORY in which I had any active part as a journalist was one that changed the course of history—the bombing of Pearl Harbor by the Japanese on December 7, 1941. It happened while I was still city editor of the *San Jose Mercury Herald,* although I was in the process of looking for another job in view of an impending change of ownership on the paper.

As it does for everyone else who was beyond childhood at the time, that terrible event remains as vivid in my memory as if it happened only yesterday. My wife and I were enjoying a leisurely late Sunday morning breakfast, a common occurrence for a morning newspaper editor who usually got home after midnight.

It was a bright, warm morning for a winter day, and we were sitting in our patio with our eighteen-month-old daughter. Through the open door to our living room we could hear the radio softly playing a symphony. As I recall, we were watching the antics of some birds on a feeder hanging from a tree and had just commented on what a beautiful day it was.

Suddenly the music stopped and a voice hoarse with emotion

broke in with words something like this: "We interrupt this program to bring you a news bulletin. The Japanese are bombing Pearl Harbor! I repeat. The Japanese are bombing Pearl Harbor!"

Not having the faintest notion where or what Pearl Harbor might be, I sat paralyzed. War, of course, was on everyone's mind in late 1941, but we were not yet really in it, and what was this?

After considerable stuttering and false starts, the radio resumed its amazing message that Japanese planes were dropping bombs on Honolulu and that there was great damage and loss of life.

At that I woke up and rushed indoors to telephone the office. A librarian was the only one on duty at the time. I told him to call in the staff, for there was hell to pay and we had a job to do. Little did I know what an enormous job that was going to be.

While scrambling into my clothes, I phoned the general manager and gave him the news. I told him that we had a clear field for an extra, since the San Francisco papers could not get an edition into San Jose for many hours, if at all that day. Also, our local rival, the *San Jose News,* doubtless would have been caught with its linotype pots cold.

(Some explanation is needed here: The electrically heated crucibles containing the molten metal used for casting type slugs in linotype machines usually were turned off to save electricity after the last edition of the newspaper had gone to press. Heating them up again took several hours. Since the *News* had put out its final edition just after noon Saturday, by Sunday noon its linotype pots would have been stone cold.

(As for the extra we were planning, such enterprises were rare on the *Mercury Herald,* which relied almost entirely on home delivery for its circulation. The San Francisco papers, still depending heavily on street sales, were apt to put out an extra any old time. In those days before Cronkite, people rushed to the newspapers to verify what they thought they had just heard on the radio, and an extra edition on an event of the magnitude of this one was not only certain to sell but was actually a public service.)

Next, I called the shop superintendent, who fortunately was home, and he said he would hurry down to round up a crew and get things started. He said he was sure a few linotype machines would have hot metal, since they were usually in use even on a Sunday morning setting advance copy for the next issue.

By the time I reached the office, some of the other members of the staff had arrived and were rushing back and forth between the clamoring telephones and the clattering teletype machines where Pearl Harbor had crowded everything else off the wire. Every phone in the place was ringing and they kept on ringing for days as people sought verification of the frequently almost hysterical radio news.

For a long time we had nothing to tell them, for the teletypes were jabbering as much nonsense as news, full of revisions and contradictions. While some of the news staff pawed through encyclopedias for information about Pearl Harbor and Manila, others tried to find maps and photos we could use. Others went out to seek sidebar features, comments from leading citizens and city officials, and to listen to dire predictions up to and including the end of the world.

I remember being trapped by one far-out caller who had found a passage in the Bible that she claimed precisely predicted just this event. She was talking so fast I could not get in a word, so I put the phone down on the desk to respond to some urgent question, and forgot all about it. Ten or fifteen minutes later somebody pointed out the neglected phone and I picked it up again. The voice was still going full speed, so I gently broke the connection, thereby no doubt passing up an important contribution to the cause.

All in all, it was early evening before we had enough usable copy to make up a front page and go to press. The rest of the four-page edition was filled with ads and yesterday's news, but we figured nobody would look at that part of the paper. People were crowding up to our front windows, where we posted hand-printed news bulletins in the manner of election returns, waiting for the extra.

I have often wished I had had the sense to save some of the teletype sheets as well as a copy of that extra, as they would make fascinating reading now. I well remember one news story that came in over the wire late in the afternoon, describing in some detail the truly frightful damage the Japanese had inflicted, only to have the story rescinded almost at once. The White House had invoked war secrecy powers to classify the material top secret, and it all had to be burned.

Not until long afterward did our readers learn what the Japanese and everybody in Hawaii had known all along—that we had lost 19 naval vessels including 8 battleships sunk or badly damaged, along with 188 aircraft and more than 2000 dead and 1100 wounded. The heart of the Pacific fleet lay in shambles and Hawaii was helpless, but for some reason that was never fully explained the Japanese sailed away.

Later I heard that some newspapers had ignored the government ban and had printed the prohibited version of the news, but that idea did not occur to us. We assumed the military had good reason for the restriction, presumably to keep the Japanese from finding out how badly they had hurt the fleet. The notion was naive, but no more so than what probably was the real reason for the action—that some of the high command in Washington were afraid the truth would be too shattering for civilian morale—an idea typical of the military mind.

Perhaps it did not matter, for what news the public did get was enough to arouse the entire nation to fever pitch overnight. The next day President Roosevelt made his famous "day of infamy" speech to Congress and the United States declared war. Not all the public reaction made sense and some of it was silly. It even seemed so at the time. I remember some vigorous veterans of World War I coming in to announce that "we'll lick those slant-eyed yellow bastards in three weeks!" They missed the mark by only three years.

It may have been some of those same crusading patriots who led the community in its thoughtless, heartless and utterly shameful crusade against the thousands of citizens of Japanese descent who had the misfortune to live in California. Whole families of people, who actually were among the most loyal of American-born citizens, were "relocated" in concentration camps in the desert, far from the coast where they presumably might have engaged in sabotage, or something.

"You can't trust any of them," and "they all look alike," were some of the glibly uttered excuses for the mass evacuation, which in all too many instances was only a shabby subterfuge for confiscating valuable property and eliminating industrious business rivals.

Most of us at the newspaper had friends among the nisei and were sickened by the relocation, but we were powerless to intervene. Had we attempted to do so, we would have been risking mob reprisal. The few stalwarts who stood up to condemn the action were shouted down, labelled "traitors" and "Jap lovers."

The cowboys were in the saddle, rounding up the Japanese just as some of their grandfathers had "taken care of the redskins," and with as much justice. Perhaps the only good aspect of the mass relocation was that it saved some fine people from direct attack by the redneck brigade. There were some ugly incidents, but no bloodshed.

All that came later. In fact, it was still going on when I left the *Mercury Herald* two months after Pearl Harbor. In the meantime, we were all too frantically busy to go crusading for any cause however worthy. As I recall, I did not get home at all for two or three days after the attack, living on coffee and sandwiches and snatching catnaps on a cot.

Now, looking back, I really do not know what all there was to do, since we were normally a single-edition newspaper and were not prepared to put out an edition every time a new story broke. But the phones continued to ring themselves crazy and all of us with them, and there seemed to be innumerable meetings to attend. There was, of course, enough news to fill half a dozen editions and the incessant demands of the Associated Press for special reports.

Situated as it is at the foot of San Francisco Bay, San Jose was and is a crossroads not only for highway and rail traffic but also for telegraph and telephone lines both north-south and east-west. If the Japanese were really intent upon attacking or even invading the coast—and there was precious little to stop them—the city would have been a prime target. Night after night we had air raid alarms and blackouts, and many a citizen went to bed with his heart in his throat.

At first, I rushed back down to the newspaper whenever one of the alarms sounded, risking my neck and the fenders of my car threading the darkened streets with headlights off. Later, the alarms became routine, and since I could do nothing about them, I learned to sleep through them.

Besides, it soon became evident that most of them were designed to get people and civilian vehicles off the streets to clear the way for rumbling convoys of tanks and other military machines that roared through the city at frequent intervals. This was before freeways, and the main highways in all directions were the main streets of the city and that was the way the convoys came, right past the front door of the newspaper. At first, we used to go out and gap at them until they, too, became routine.

There also was some reason to think the Japanese might attack the coast, if not invade it, at least on a raid. Rumor crowded on rumor of sightings of submarines off the coast, then two weeks after Pearl Harbor a Japanese submarine surfaced and shelled a Richfield Oil tanker off Monterey Bay, no more than forty miles from San Jose and in plain sight of watchers on the higher hills. Having no gun crew, the tanker attempted to ram the submarine while the crew pelted the enemy vessel with potatoes. The tanker then made its zig-zag way to safety in heavy seas.

On the same day, another submarine torpedoed the tanker *Emidio* several hundred miles up the coast, with a loss of five lives. Still later, the Japanese launched fire balloons off the coast into easterly winds in an only partly successful attempt to start forest fires in Oregon.

Not long after Pearl Harbor some of the younger members

of the news staff began to leave, some into war-related industries, some to larger newspapers, some to military commissions. One of my top reporters became the captain of a gun crew on a freighter which later was torpedoed, but not sunk, in the South Pacific, and another wound up patrolling the coast in a small dirigible.

I was not very long in following them out of San Jose.

29

THE PHONY PHOTO
(Seven Months in the Big Time)

PROBABLY THE DREAM of every young Western country newspaperman in the 1930s was to get a job on a San Francisco newspaper, the "big time" for aspiring journalists anywhere north of San Luis Obispo. South of there they headed for Los Angeles and Hollywood.

It took me thirteen years and a little help from World War II to get there, to what turned out to be by all odds the worst newspaper job I ever had after I left Pleasanton. I was thirty-three years old at the time, married with one child and another on the way, which made me reasonably draft-proof for the time being.

The *San Jose Mercury Herald,* where I had been serving as city editor, had just been sold to a chain and combined with the rival *San Jose News.* Especially in the editorial departments, we could feel the sharp edge of the axe poised over some of our necks, most especially mine. I was not exactly popular with the publishers because of my Guild activities, among other things.

Through a friend on the *San Francisco News,* I wangled an interview with the managing editor of that Scripps-Howard sheet, then running a poor fourth to the two Hearst papers and the *San Francisco Chronicle.*

The managing editor, I soon learned, was an odd character given to taking up the first half hour of each day's working time with play-by-play accounts of his previous night's conquests. Then he usually took a nap for an hour or two in the library.

I got the job without much fuss, fully aware that the war had drained away just about every able-bodied newspaperman under fifty in town, most of all from the *News.* The job was on what is known as the Rim, the horse-shoe desk where the copy editors sat, editing and writing heads on the day's outpouring.

It did not take me long to discover that I had made one of the worst decisions in my working life. I do not recall ever before or since going to work every day with a baseball-sized cold lump in my middle. Without describing all the gory details, suffice it to say that if this was big-time journalism, I wanted no part of it. I was disillusioned in a week, jaundiced in a month.

I remember the circulation manager coming up to the editorial department to pound on the desk and shout that he could not sell bad news, so how about printing some "good" war news? In 1942 this was, when, if you recall, the Allies were losing on every hand and in every theater of the war.

So we printed "good" news. If a company of Marines surprised a Japanese cook and two dish washers in a jungle camp, we headlined it as a major victory. If we lost an aircraft carrier in the South Pacific, it wound up on page six. I am exaggerating, of course, but not very much.

Almost as bad, journalistically speaking, was the chore assigned to our meager little staff of reporters and rewrite men. For the first hour or so every day they had to pound out some of those pernicious little paragraphs known as "business office musts." These dreary little blurbs of free advertising were promised as a bonus to merchants silly enough to buy space in our rag. They were about almost anything from the opening of a shoe store on the wrong side of Market Street to the arrival of a new hairdresser in a Telegraph Hill botique. Mind you, this was in war time, when paper was scarce and we rarely had enough space to cover the great amount of news coming off the wires.

As a copyreader, I found I could do away with quite a lot of this junk by burying it under the pile of papers on the desk, and then letting some of it slide off into the wastebasket if nobody asked about it for a few days. The place was so disorganized nobody ever seemed to know where anything was anyhow.

In fairness, I should mention that it was not all grief and gloom on the *News*. As soon as the boss went home, just after lunch on Saturdays, the weekly game of seven-up (ten-cent limit) got under way. The paper kept a skeleton staff around until late in the day, but in all the time I was there we never did anything but play poker.

One Saturday our man at City Hall called in, as he was obliged to do every half hour, to report that the gang in the press room had a gimmick going. They had called up the state liquor control director, a freewheeling politician known for his flamboyant gestures at the taxpayers' expense, and told him it was the anniversary of the birth of the founder of American journalism, none other than Booker T. Washington.

Although it was his day off, the politico responded as the city hall bunch hoped he would, to help out with the celebration then in progress in the press room. He sent around a case of good whiskey, very hard to come by in World War II. From then on the half-hourly reports from our man at City Hall became progressively more confused and finally stopped entirely about midafternoon.

The *Time* magazine reporter, who was among those present, betrayed his fellows by running a facetious account of the event in his magazine a week or two later. We all thought that had killed the goose, so as to speak, but we were wrong. I heard later that the celebration was repeated the following year with equal success and may, for all I know, still be going on. Politicians take no chances, it seems.

I never did find out whether that actually was Booker T. Washington's birthday; I think it was more like the birthday of that other Washington. By this time I had already decided to get out of there as soon as I could. For one thing, my draft board had hinted that it would be happier if I were to get a job in some essential industry, which the *San Francisco News* clearly was not.

Then there came the episode of the phony photo.

As low man on the totem pole, I was left alone on the copydesk at noon, when everybody else went out to lunch. (This was fine with me, because I brought my lunch in an old-fashioned lunch bucket, and was therefore scorned by the rest of the staff for doing so. They let me know they preferred to pay outrageous prices for an indigestible meal at a nearby ptomaine parlor rather than submit to the indignity of carrying a workingman's pail.)

One noon I received a phone call from Acme Photo Service, the Scripps-Howard wire photo office on the next floor. The man said he had "another one of those phony Japanese propaganda pictures about the Bataan death march." Did I want it for the final edition, or should he send it down with the overnight stuff? I told him to send it later and thought no more about it.

Unfortunately, the rival afternoon paper, the Hearst *Call-Bulletin,* chose to splash the same photo over the front page of its green sheet, its home edition feature section.

(For background, let me explain that each newspaper had a copyboy hovering around the other's press room to rush back copies of each edition as it came out. Believe it or not, without regard to the news value involved, each paper would then replate the front page to match the headlines of the other. Once in a while both headlined the same story in the same edition, which saved a lot of trouble.)

My first intimation that all was not peaceful in paradise came when the editor in chief, a cold and secretive man who rarely left his office, came storming out to the copy desk with the *Call-Bulletin* green sheet clutched in his fist.

"How did this happen?" he demanded to know. By then I knew enough to sit tight. It was like a ringside seat at a fixed fight where I knew who was going to lose.

Somebody called up Acme and learned that the photo had been offered to us at noon. The next question, who was on the desk at noon? I was. All eyes turned in my direction.

When asked directly, I replied that I had indeed turned down the photo because I didn't think it was worth running, having been advised by Acme that it was a Japanese propaganda picture.

I'm not really sure what might have happened next had it not been for my old friend Chet Johnson, who had been around long enough to know how to create a diversion. He also was the only good rewrite man the *News* had and was all but indispensable, and he knew it.

He ambled over to the copy desk and at the crucial moment said, "For Christ's sake, what's all the rumpus about? That picture was in the *Saturday Evening Post* a month ago and it's been kicking around ever since."

Without a word, the editor in chief turned on his heel and went back to his office, I guess to sulk. Later, in the washroom, I thanked Chet and remarked that I had not seen the photo in the *Post*.

"Neither did I," he grinned.

The *News* ran the photo the next day, just in case, and I went looking for another job. As I mentioned, the draft board had suggested that it would be happier if I were in a war industry, so that is where I went.

And with just one exception, I did not return to newspaper writing as a full-time occupation for twenty-five years.

30

NEW JOBS

EVEN SO ABBREVIATED a biography as this one should not have to leap over a quarter century without a pause, even though it took me that long to get back into the writing game as a full-time occupation.

When I quit the *San Francisco News* in the fall of 1942 to go into a war industry, it was partly at the urging of my draft board, but mostly because I was completely fed up with big city journalism. However, it was not very long before I found myself temporarily back in the role of a reporter, and this is how it came about:

Before I burned my bridges in San Francisco, I had lined up a job as an electrical draftsman for a small company that manufactured critical components for military radar. At the time, of course, I did not know that, since the very word "radar" was top secret. I got the job through a friend who had been retreaded from a newspaper linotypist to a machinist, one of the ninety-day wonders that World War II turned out in such amazing numbers in such a hurry. He told me there was an opening for a draftsman at his place of employment (which I had never heard of) and arranged for an interview.

That was not so brash a venture as might seem for a refugee from the city room. I had built radio sets as a boy, worked as an electrician's helper, took a correspondence course in applied electricity, and had taken a lot of drafting in high school. All that was when I still thought I wanted to be an engineer.

I could draw fairly well and understood electrical symbols; I could even tell a voltmeter from a velocipede. The company did not really want an electrical engineer, even if any had been available, but somebody who knew just enough to draw circuit diagrams from rough notes and from out of other people's heads. Since the company was working far beyond the state of the art, the usual handbooks were useless. The circuits I was to draw came from fertile imaginations or sheer desperation and were scrawled on the backs of envelopes or on scratch paper; many existed nowhere outside the weird and wonderful equipment they operated.

My job was to track down the circuits from whatever source and get them down on paper in a hurry. That's why it was as much a job for a reporter as for a draftsman. I had to find the individuals who had the information, hold them by the shirttails long enough to talk to me, and cajole them into giving me what I needed. I spent a hectic week once with a flashlight and a helper inside a boxcar, tracing out the circuits in a huge piece of equipment about to be shipped to Salt Lake City, where the company was opening a new plant.

I should mention that the company was Eitel-McCullough, Inc., of San Bruno. Its trade name was Eimac and its product known as Eimac tubes. The firm long ago was absorbed by Varian at San Carlos, but the Eimac brand is still widely known in the electronics field and to amateur radio operators everywhere.

The tubes, or valves as the British call them, were the electronic predecessors of transistors, and in World War II they powered all radio and radar transmitters and receivers. When I went to work for Eimac, it was the sole supplier of most types of radar transmitting tubes for the Western alliance. Like most war industries its work never stopped, around the clock, seven days a week.

I had been there several weeks when I met two men in rapid succession who had a lot to do with what happened to me next and for years to come.

The first was a man about my age, in dungarees like almost everyone else in the plant. I encountered him in the basement where I worked. We stopped and gaped at one another, and then said in unison, "Hey! I know you. Weren't you in Los Gatos high school when I was?" Or words to that effect.

He said his name was Bill Eitel. I remembered him as a classmate who had been too busy with his hobby as a ham radio operator to attend his own graduation in 1926.

"Are you any relation to the guy who owns this place?" I asked. He grinned and nodded. "The same," he said, and that was that.

My next encounter was with none other than E. J. Demson, the former *Mercury Herald* general manager. I had not seen or heard from him since he left the paper soon after Pearl Harbor. In the uniform of a Navy lieutenant commander, he visited the plant regularly on his job with the office of naval procurement.

His mission, he told me, was to keep the company going by whatever means it took—financial or otherwise. Draft deferments for irreplaceable young technicians (like glass-blowing–lathe operators) were among his major responsibilities.

So I guess I was not surprised when I was suddenly called away from my drawing board to write job descriptions in support of draft deferment applications. In this I could see Demson's hand and Eitel's concurrence. It was straight reporting again. Nothing was written down anywhere about the jobs, since the company had burgeoned from 17 employees to around 3000 in a matter of months. I had to interview the men on the job, shouting over the roar of the equipment and dodging flames and whirling machinery, any time I could find them day or night, and try to figure out what they were doing.

It was much harder, physically, than any news reporting I had ever done but much easier otherwise since there was absolutely no reluctance on the part of the men to give me the data and no hard-boiled city editor to chop up my copy.

Next, since I had long ago lost any awe of brass, especially military brass, I was sent to Sacramento to argue with the state director of selective service, who happened to be a retired general. This step was necessary since none of the local draft boards were cleared for top secret information and anyhow probably could not have understood why a manufacturer of radar equipment (whatever that was) had to have a couple of dozen glass-lathe operators (whatever they might be).

I felt quite sure that the general, a formidable gentleman with a ramrod spine, a chest plastered with decorations, and a highly suspicious nature, did not know what I was talking about. I think he was more impressed by Demson, who came with me for moral support, than by my presentation. In any case, we got the deferments.

After the flurry of draft deferments, I was back at my drawing board one morning when I was summoned to the front office. There I found Demson, along with Bill Eitel, Jack McCullough, Hank Brown, George Wunderlich and some other members of the top management, all sitting around a conference table. It was the first time I had met some of them and the only time I ever saw them all together, since they usually were running around the plant in a frenzy.

Eitel opened the ball. "We understand that you do not approve of the way we are running this place," he announced.

For a moment I was stunned. Then I realized that Demson had been up to his tricks. We both lived in Palo Alto, where Demson was renting a house on the Stanford campus from a physics professor on leave. (That is not an irrelevant fact, as will later develop). From time to time my wife and I had dinner with the Demsons, and

I had mentioned to Demson some possible trouble spots at Eimac. They were all the result of too rapid growth, but nonetheless threatening. As a draftsman in the construction department, I heard a lot of griping and from my newspaper Guild experience recognized its validity.

It was not so much a matter of the level of wages, which were about par on the average, but some gross inequities that had grown up within the structure—or the lack of any structure at all. There also was no published policy covering such fringe benefits as sick leave, vacations, shift premiums and the like. The management was actually extremely liberal, but haphazard. Everybody had been much too busy keeping up production around the clock to worry about details like personnel policies.

This, among other things, was what I had been telling Demson, and obviously it was what he had passed on to Eitel and McCullough. It was also immediately apparent that I had not been called in to be scolded, but to be pumped for information. So, taking a deep breath, I summed up for the group what I had told Demson and then some.

"How bad is it?" one of them wanted to know.

"Bad enough that I believe I could organize a union in your plant in a matter of days," I replied. "As a matter of fact, I know that several Bay area unions are already interested." I had nothing against unions as such but felt that they were not needed in this situation and that the management was singularly ill-prepared to deal with a jurisdictional dispute. I told them that also.

"Can you fix it?" was the next question.

"Who, me?" I asked in amazement. "You've got the wrong guy. Remember, I'm a draftsman down in construction."

I think it was Bill Eitel who then asked, "Could you do it if you were personnel director?"

I laughed. "I don't know anything about personnel work," I replied. "I've just had a little experience on the labor side."

"Well, you've been talking a good line. How about putting it into action?" Eitel said, and I realized all the cards were on the table.

I blinked a few times and looked at Demson. He was sitting there with his usual Cheshire cat smile, and I surmised that he had not only planted the seed but had thoroughly watered the plant.

"When would you want me to start?" I asked.

"You have already started, this morning," was the answer. And in three years that was the only management meeting I ever attended. I went to Stanford at night for a month or two to take some ESMWT (Emergency Science and Management War Training) courses but found them a waste of time. Then I tore around to other war plants and picked the brains of their personnel experts. I also stole a couple of their people.

While all this was going on, I was on a crash program to develop those fringe benefits and publish an employee's handbook to spell them out, the last another job for a reporter. I also started an in-plant magazine and wrote most of it until I could train an employee-editor. Then I had to develop a comprehensive wage and salary system to meet the stringent requirements of the federal wage stabilization laws on the one hand and to get wages high enough to keep highly trained people. I often worked seven or more twelve-hour days in a row, but so did everybody else at Eimac.

It all turned out to be the groundwork in the next step in my erratic career, over which I never seemed to have any control.

I had noticed that I had not seen Demson around for some weeks. The front office (and his wife) said he was out of town on a special mission, and I asked no further. Then one day I met him on the commuter train we both usually used. He did not say where he had been, but I knew he was up to something.

About that time came the news of the atomic bombs being dropped on Japan and the end of the war. Then Demson could tell me that he had been at Los Alamos, New Mexico, where the bombs were developed. The physics professor from whom Demson was renting his house at Stanford was Dr. Norris E. Bradbury, who was appointed in September, 1945, to succeed Dr. J. Robert Oppenheimer as director of the Los Alamos Scientific Laboratory, then and now operated by the University of California.

Faced with the job of setting up an entire new administration, Bradbury sent for Demson, whom he had met several times on quick trips home. Demson, in turn, sent for me to help him with the personnel end. He was mainly concerned with developing a wage and salary and fringe benefit structure to replace the hodgepodge that had served during the war. It was Eimac all over again, at least for me, but an Eimac on a high plateau up in the Rocky Mountains of northern New Mexico.

I went there, on a military plane, on about two hours' notice, to serve as a consultant on a thirty-day leave of absence from Eimac. I never went back to Eimac except for a farewell visit, and a month later I moved my family to the strange, closely guarded compound that was Los Alamos in late 1945. Why? I guess because it was an exciting challenge in an entirely new world. My job at Eimac was running out, anyhow, as the company was rapidly shrinking to a more normal postwar operation.

Like the war years at Eimac, the next twenty-two years that I spent at Los Alamos would make another book. Exciting it was, especially in the early years, rubbing shoulders with world-famous figures. Our next-door neighbor in our first four-family apartment was Enrico Fermi. I met Oppenheimer, Edward Teller, John von Neumann, Hans Bethe and scores of others well known in the scientific fraternity.

After eight years as personnel director at Los Alamos, I was asked by Bradbury to set up a public relations department, primarily to meet the increasing need for public information about what was going on in that mysterious place. The town had been open to ordinary traffic for several years, but to most of the nation, including the taxpayers who were supporting it, it was still a secret city.

A good part of my new job, especially at first, was to try to convince the public that (1) New Mexico was and is one of the United States; (2) entry to Los Alamos required neither a passport nor a vaccination certificate; and (3) that it was situated high up in the mountains and not down by White Sands amid the horned toads.

Then there were constant battles with the Washington bureaucracy, particularly the staff of the Atomic Energy Commission, who wanted to monkey with news releases to make them shed a favorable light on the government regardless of whose baby it was. Since my mandate from the laboratory director was to "get it into print, the sooner the better" provided the story was decent and unclassified, some hairy encounters ensued.

Fortunately, the effort to control the news did *not* extend to the Regents of the University of California at Berkeley. All they asked was that they be informed, if possible, of important events before they hit the front pages of the San Francisco newspapers, or the radio, in order that they might have some answers when queried.

One of the few times I got into trouble with Berkeley occurred when several children were injured, one fatally, by a bazooka shell left over from World War II which exploded while they were playing with it at home in Los Alamos. The incident had nothing to do with the laboratory or the University as such, but that made no difference either to the press or to the Regents when the phones started to jump off their desks.

After that, whenever anything even remotely connected with Los Alamos seemed likely to hit the wires, I made a valiant effort to get there first with a phone call, even in the middle of the night, to my friend and mentor, Robert E. Underhill, longtime secretary-treasurer of the University's Board of Regents. He never scolded me for calling him, no matter when or about what—only when I failed to do so. Never in the eight years I was on that job did he, or anyone else at the University level, ever make any effort to control or edit any news release from our end.

Although I was not aware of it at the time, the public relations job was nudging me back toward journalism, willy-nilly. I do not think I had any notion of starting a new career in mind when I took the next step—what appeared to me at the time to be simply a bit of spare-time work that might make me a few odd dollars.

On the spur of the moment late in 1964, I sent a free-lance travel article, with a couple of photos, to the *New York Times* Sunday travel and resorts section, which I had been reading for some time. Earlier, I had had a few short pieces accepted by magazines and one or two newspapers, but nothing at the level of the *Times*. When the article was accepted and published, I was off and running.

A year and a half later, in mid-1966, I had developed enough markets for free-lance articles and photos to persuade myself to quit the University and go to work full-time for myself, full-circle back to the writing game.

Somewhere along the line I remember the historical articles I had written for the *San Jose Mercury Herald* as a country reporter back in 1934. I no longer had any copies of those articles, but an old friend, Roger Clark, then chief librarian at the *Mercury Herald*, sent me a full set of photostats of the series. I extracted material from two or three of the articles for use in the *New York Times*.

Thus, when several friends insisted that I should make the articles into a book, I had the stories at hand. *Ghost Towns of the Santa Cruz Mountains* was published in book form by Paper Vision Press of Santa Cruz in December, 1979, and I found myself in the business of writing books, like this one.

INDEX